top touring spots in
South Africa

Roger de la Harpe

SUNBIRD PUBLISHING

First published 2002
2 4 6 8 10 9 7 5 3 1
Sunbird Publishing (Pty) Ltd, 34 Sunset Avenue, Llandudno, Cape Town, South Africa
Registration number: 4850177827

Publisher Dick Wilkins
Editor Peter Joyce
Designer Mandy McKay
Production Manager Andrew de Kock

Reproduction by Unifoto (Pty) Ltd, Cape Town
Printed and bound by Tien Wah Press (Pte) Ltd, Singapore

ISBN 0 624 03950 1

ACKNOWLEDGMENTS

The author and photographer thank the following individuals, enterprises and institutions for their hospitality, help and unfailing courtesy in the preparation of this book.

MPUMALANGA

Golden Monkey Tourism/Big 5 Central Reservations, Sabie, tel: 013 737 8191; goldenm@mweb.co.za
Nelspruit Info, Nelspruit, tel: 013 7555 1988/9; nelspruit@parks-sa.co.za
Gleighnelly's Country Lodge, White River, tel: 013 751 1100; glenelly@glenelly.co.za
Bohm's Zeederberg Country House, Sabie, tel: 013 737 8101; bohms@mweb.co.za
Tim and Kim Buckland, Riverbend Farm
Bike Doc, Sabie, tel: 013 764 1034; denzilbikedoc@xsinet.co.za
Injabula Restaurant, Greenway Woods Hotel and Conference Centre, White River, tel: 013 751 1094
Mount Anderson, Lydenburg, tel: 031 765 2900; reservations@malamala.com
Mala Mala Game Reserve, tel: 031 765 2900; reservations@malamala.com
Moholoholo Wildlife Rehabilitation Centre, Hoedspruit, tel: 015 795 5236; moholorehab@wol.co.za
Hoedspruit Research and Breeding Centre, Hoedspruit, tel: 015 7931633
Kapama Lodge and Camps, Hoedspruit, tel: 015 793 1038; gentour@iafrica.com
Scenic Helicopter Flights, Hazyview, tel: 013 741 4651; henkb@nac.co.za
The Royal Hotel, Pilgrim's Rest, tel: 013 768 1100; royal@mweb.co.za
Kaapschehoop Conference Centre, Kaapschehoop, tel: 013 734 4161; roelfjw@mweb.co.za
Silver Mist Guest House, Kaapschehoop tel: 013 734 4429, cell 082 860 4824
Koek 'n Pan Pancake Corner, Kaapschehoop, cell 082 601 5455
Kaapschehoop Horse Trails, tel: 013 734 4995, cell 082 774 5826
Eureka City Ghost Town Tours, Barberton, tel: 013 712 5055, cell 082 933 9565
Fountain Baths Guest House, Barberton, tel: 013 712 2707; fountainbaths@hotmail.com

GARDEN ROUTE AND KLEIN KAROO

Thatchwood Country Lodge, St Francis Bay, tel: 042 294 0082; thatchwood@intekom.co.za
St Francis Tourism, St Francis Bay, tel: 042 294 0076; stfrantr@intekom.co.za
Tsitsikamma Lodge, Storms River, tel: 042 7503802; info@tsitsikamma.com
Hog Hollow Country Lodge, Plettenberg Bay, tel: 044 534 8769; info@hog-hollow.com
Keurbooms River Lodge, Keurbooms, tel: 044 534 8906
Keurbooms River Ferries, Keurbooms, tel: 044 532 7876; ferry@ferry.co.za
Garden Route Lodge, Plettenberg Bay, tel: 044 534 8837; grlodge@lantic.net
Monkeyland Primate Sanctuary: tel: 044 534 8906; monkeys@global.co.za
The Knysna River Club, Knysna, tel: 042 382 6483
Knysna Log Inn, Knysna, tel: 044 382 5835; logg-inn@mweb.co.za
Ashmead Resort, Knysna, tel: 044 384 1166; ashmead@pixie.co.za
Hunter's Country House, Plettenberg Bay, tel: 044 532 7818; reservations@hunterhotels.com
The Cheese Farm, Tsitsikamma, tel: 042 280 3879
African Ramble Air Charter, Knysna, tel: 044 533 9006; aframble@cis.co.za
Stanley Island Glider Flights, Keurbooms, tel: 044 535 9442; bhbecke@global.co.za
Seal Adventures, Knysna, tel: 044 3810068; seals@mweb.co.za
Gorah Elephant Camp, Addo Elephant Park, tel: 044 532 7818; res@hunterhotels.com
The Phantom Forest Eco Reserve, Knysna, tel: 044 386 0046; phantomforest@mweb.co.za
Knysna Oyster Company, Knysna, tel: 044 382 6941
Knysna Township Tours, Knysna, cell 082 925 0716; ecoafrik@imaginet.co.za
Knysna Elephant Park, Knysna, tel: 044 532 7732; kep@pixie.co.za
Brother's Restaurant, Plettenberg Bay, tel: 044 533 5056
Bitou River Lodge, Plettenberg Bay, tel: 044 535 9577; info@bitou.co.za
Kon Tours, George, cell 082 569 8997
Fancourt Hotel and Country Club Estate, George, tel: 044 804 0000; hotel@fancourt.co.za
Forest and Mountain Tours, Plettenberg Bay, tel: 042 2811 015; fmtours@cyberperk.co.za
Kleinplaas Accommodation, Oudtshoorn, tel: 044 272 5811; kleinpls@mweb.co.za

Kobus se Gat, tel: 044 279 1831; swartexp@mweb.co.za
Storms River Adventures, Storms River, tel: 042 541 1836; adventure@gardenroute.co.za
Bloukrans Bungee, Bloukrans Bridge, tel: 042 2811458; bungy@global.co.za
Ocean Safaris, Plettenberg Bay, tel: 044 533 4963, cell 082 784 5729; info@oceansafaris.co.za
Grootbos Nature Reserve, Gansbaai, tel: 028 384 0381, email grootbos@hermanus.co.za
De Bergkant Lodge and Cottages, Prince Albert, tel: 023 541 1088; bergkant@iafrica.com
Safari Ostrich Farm, Oudtshoorn, tel: 044 272 7311/2; safariostrich@mweb.co.za
Jemima's Restaurant, Oudtshoorn, tel: 044 272 0808,
Marine Dynamics Shark Expeditions, Gansbaai, tel: 028 384 1005; jpb@iafrica.com
Huijs te Marquette, Mossel Bay, tel: 044 691 3182; marquette@pixie.co.za
Shark Africa, Mossel Bay, cell 082 455 2438; sharkafrica@mweb.co.za
Lisa Price Tours, Mossel Bay, tel: 044 698 1320, cell 082 473 9264

CAPE TOWN

Beth and Doug Howieson
Bo-Kaap Guided Tours, Cape Town, tel: 021 422 1554, cell 082 423 6932
Robben Island Museum, Robben Island, tel: 021 419 1300

KWAZULU-NATAL

Ezimvelo KZN Wildlife, Pietermaritzburg, tel: 033 845 1000; bookings@kznwildlife.com
Sani Pass Hotel, tel: 033 702 1320; info@sanipasshotel.co.za
Ardmore Guest Farm, Winterton, tel: 036 468 1314; ardmore@futurenet.co.za
Tourism KZN, Durban, tel: 031 304 7144; tkzn@iafrica.com
Isibindi Africa, Umhlali, tel: 035 474 1504; isibindi@iafrica.com
Rocktail Bay Lodge, Kosi Bay, tel: 011 8071800; enquiry@wilderness.co.za
Zimbali Country Club, Ballito, tel: 032 538 1041; zimbali@sunint.co.za
Umgeni River Bird Park, Durban, tel: 031 579 4600; urbpmark@iafrica.com
Sea World, Durban, tel: 031 337 3536; seaworld@dbn.lia.net
Sharks Board, Umhlanga, tel: 031 566 0400; hargreaves@shark.co.za

FREE STATE

Meiringkloof Nature Reserve, Fouriesburg, tel: 058 223 0067 Lou and Deon van Reenen
Dinosaur and Fossil Hunting Trails, Clarens, cell 082 829 4978; gideonppf@bhm.dorea.co.za
Sunflower Tours, Ladybrand, tel: 051 924 5131; malotiinfo@xsinet.co.za

GAUTENG

Gaye and Bruce Dorkin
The Sun City Resort, Pilanesberg, tel: 014 557 1020; sityres@sunint.co.za
Gametrackers, Pilanesberg Game Reserve, tel: 014 552 1561 ext. 583
Tshukudu Lodge, Pilanesberg Game Reserve, tel: 014 552 6255; tshukudu@legacyhotels.kosa.co.za

EASTERN CAPE

African Coastal Adventures, tel: 043 748 4550; aca@africoast.co.za
Cremorne Estate, Port St Johns, tel: 047 564 1110/3; info@cremorne.co.za
Umngazi River Bungalows, tel: 047 564 1115/6; umngazi@iafrica.com
Morgan's Bay Hotel, Morgan's Bay, tel: 043 841 1062; mb.hotel@mweb.co.za
Trennery's Hotel, Wild Coast, tel: 047 498 0095
Kob Inn Hotel, Wild Coast, tel: 047 4990011; mwkobinn@iafrica.com
Ocean View Hotel, Coffee Bay, tel: 047 575 2005/6; oceanview@coffeebay.co.za
Algoa Grand Prix, Port Elizabeth, tel: 041 487 3981
The Boardwalk Casino and Entertainment World, Port Elizabeth, tel: 041 507 7777; boardwalk@sunint.co.za
Bayworld Oceanarium, Port Elizabeth, tel: 041 5861051; sandy@bayworld.co.za
King's Tide Boutique Hotel, Port Elizabeth, tel: 041 583 6023; kingstide@crowncollection.co.za
Board Room Sand Boarding, Port Elizabeth, tel: 041 586 2276, cell 083 735 4865
Shamwari Game Reserve, tel: 042 203 1111; shamwaribooking@global.co.za
Grahamstown Tourism, Grahamstown, tel: 046 622 3241; info@grahamstown.co.za

HALF-TITLE PAGE *Guests at Kosi Forest Lodge watch waterfowl as they arrive to roost at sunset.*
TITLE PAGE *Table Mountain forms a backdrop to Murray's Bay, Robben Island's only sandy beach.*
OPPOSITE *The 11th hole on The Links Course at Fancourt Golfing Estate, at the base of the beautiful Outeniqua Mountains.*

Contents

Introduction

ABOVE Cape Town's Waterfront: a major tourist attraction in a splendid setting.
BELOW A heavyweight resident of the Eastern Cape's Addo Elephant Park.
BOTTOM RIGHT Looking out over Kaapschehoop, near Barberton in eastern Mpumalanga.

We are extremely fortunate in that, during the course of our work, we have had the opportunity to travel extensively, not only around South Africa (covering vast areas), but elsewhere in Africa and, indeed, occasionally to other continents as well. What our foreign travel has brought home to us is that South Africa is not only a visually stunning country but an exciting one as well, with a rich and invigorating mix of people, cultures, scenery and wildlife.

And even better, it is a very easy country in which to get around. There

is a good network of well-signposted roads, a sufficient number of airports and a reasonable rail network, all comparable to any First World region. Yet there are still areas where it is possible to get lost for days, where people still live as they have done in bygone eras and where wild animals roam.

Perhaps the most enjoyable part of our travels was the discovery of an overwhelming number of people involved in the tourism industry who are committed to and positive about South Africa. On one trip alone we spoke to many who spanned the economic and racial spectrum and included, to mention just a handful: a wealthy landowner who was building a number of very up-market guesthouses, the Director General of one of the provincial tourism departments who was out there moving and shaking and getting things done, a family setting up a small touring company, and the residents of a tiny, impoverished Overberg village who were intent on learning about how to launch, and successfully run, several bed-and-breakfast establishments. Bumping up against people with such optimistic sentiments certainly made our various excursions into different parts of the country a valuable personal experience.

Our trips also revealed numerous interesting destinations and experiences

that are not included in the average tourist itinerary, opportunities to see and feel the unusual, the different and the quirky. The 4x4 safaris along the Eastern Cape's Wild Coast, run by African Coastal Adventures, spring to mind, as does Grundheim Distillery, located just outside Oudtshoorn and owned by a seventh-generation Afrikaner family. Then there is the restaurant, situated halfway up the Swartberg Pass, known as Kobus se Gat, with its delicious potjiekos and 'sakkie sakkie' dance floor, the motorised glider flights at Plettenberg Bay and the Turtle Tours along the Maputaland coast. The list goes on.

And so the idea for the book was born. A book dealing with the finest that South Africa has to offer in the way of tourism. Not the most popular places (although some of the spots that we have included are very popular) and not the most expensive (although one or two of the destinations are very expensive) but what we consider to be the very best. This has, of course, made the book very subjective, and there are bound to be differing opinions about what constitutes the top touring spots – but these are our own choices, and they are based on our own experiences.

We have arranged the book in a series of routes that, essentially, wind their way successively through the eastern, southern and western parts of the country. The

great majority of them require no more than the average family sedan, but there are a few destinations that need a four-wheel-drive for comfortable access. The Richtersveld is one such, as are certain parts of Maputaland and some of the trails in the Kgalagadi Transfrontier Park.

We trust that you will find the venues, and see the sights, as easily as we did, and that they are as enjoyable and as exciting for you as they were for us when we put this book together.

ROGER DE LA HARPE, PHOTOGRAPHER

ABOVE The limpid, oyster-rich waters of the Knysna Lagoon, on South Africa's southern seaboard.
BELOW Hippo and friend in the Mkhuze Game Reserve, northern KwaZulu-Natal.

Far Horizons

Pilgrim's Rest and Blyde River Canyon

First-time visitors tend to rush through the Lowveld in their hurry to get to the Kruger National Park – which is a pity, because there is a lot to see and enjoy en route. Even though the area has been heavily developed for agriculture and there are enormous commercial forestry plantations, it is still very beautiful in most parts, and the roads are excellent. Many lovely rivers rise in the mountains; no fewer than eight waterfalls tumble over the Escarpment, and a myriad smaller ones grace the exquisite valleys.

Pilgrim's Rest and Blyde River Canyon

Nelspruit, White River, Sabie, Graskop, Pilgrim's Rest, Hazyview, Blyde River Canyon, Mount Anderson, Waterval-Boven and Waterval-Onder, Sudwala Caves and Dinosaur Park, Barberton

Steeped in a past that spans the long millennia from the age of the dinosaurs right through to the gold-rush of the late 1800s, the area surrounding Pilgrim's Rest and the Blyde River Canyon is one of both mystery and breathtaking beauty. Some of the most spectacular views in Africa unfold from the heights of the Escarpment.

TOP The escarpment at Kaapschehoop drops down into the plains of the beautiful De Kaap Crater Valley.
ABOVE Kaapschehoop's wild horses roam free, often moving right into the town.
PREVIOUS PAGES The Eland's River Falls, just outside Waterval Boven, are especially spectacular after rains.

NELSPRUIT

Nelspruit is the main business centre of the Lowveld, and the gateway to the Kruger National Park. Its small international airport is the busiest rural airport in South Africa, and services the two neighbouring states of Mozambique and Swaziland as well as the Kruger.

Lowveld National Botanical Garden

Nelspruit can be terribly hot and muggy, and a visit to the wonderfully cool Lowveld National Botanical Garden, on the banks of the Crocodile River, provides a refreshingly welcome respite. The Garden lies on the outskirts of town, on the way to White River. Dry though it tends to be in winter, the Garden is always attractive – and always fascinating. A number of walking trails lead around the area, a couple of which take you to the two waterfalls, another to the enchanting tropical forest, whose residents include some massive and strangely shaped fig trees. The cycad garden is especially interesting: these 'living fossils' claim an origin that predates the dinosaurs. Once prolific in the area, cycads are now greatly reduced in number and distribution, and some have become very rare indeed. There is a small café in the Garden where light lunches and teas are served.

Kaapschehoop

Perched in the hills above Nelspruit, among the gnarled and twisted rocks

10

on the edge of the mountains overlooking the magnificent De Kaap crater valley (or Death Valley, as it is sometimes known), is the tiny town of Kaapschehoop.

Kaapschehoop has known its days of glory. In the later years of the 19th century it became the centre of a frenetic gold rush and by 1910 served as home to some 2 000 families. Even though mining activities slowly petered out in the early 1900s, the town, with its mining commissioner, post office service and police force, remained a major Lowveld centre of activity until as late as 1958.

Today, this hospitable, pretty little village is well known for its rare blue swallows and weird rock formations, and for its wild horses, an estimated 130 to 170 of which roam the surrounding hills and dales. One of the best ways to see the horses, as well as the forests, waterfalls and spectacular vistas of the area, is on horseback (that is, on a tame horse!). Kaapschehoop Horse Trails runs splendid pony camps; on offer are day rides, weekend and wilderness trails, both catered and self-catered.

The village itself consists of a number of the original buildings, some of which have been restored. One has been turned into a restaurant/pancake house; another – Silver Mist – now serves as a gracious guest house. There's also general accommodation and a small conference centre in the village.

An excellent local guide is available to show you around and fill you in on area's history and environment.

WHITE RIVER
Rottcher Wineries

Rottcher is a winery with a difference. The vintages produced here are not made from grapes, but from the oranges that grow in such abundance in the fields of the Lowveld. You can tour the winery, see how they process their unusual product, and take part in a wine-tasting session. One of the most popular of the wines is that made from orange and ginger. The farm and winery complex, which has been in operation for generations, also incorporates the Nutcracker Valley nut factory, which exports most of its output. Also worth touring is the nearby macadamia nut farm. If you haven't the

time to tour, call in at the farmstall, where Rottcher wines and nuts are on sale. The entrance to the farmstall is paved in nutshells.

Butterfly Park

South Africa is home to a great diversity of butterfly species, many of them both unusual and visually stunning, and in recent years increased interest in these creatures has prompted the creation of a number of butterfly gardens around the country. Just outside White River, and attached to a plant and herb nursery, is one such – an especially attractive little park where hundreds of these colourful creatures flit freely among the flowers. Tours are laid on, during which the guide will tell you all about the various species. After the walkabout, one can sit at leisure among the plants and enjoy the splendid array.

SABIE

The small centre of Sabie nestles among the foothills of Mount Anderson. Developed for the most part to serve the timber industry – the largest sawmill in the country is just outside town, at Ngodwana – Sabie is surrounded by scenic splendour and great green expanses of commercial forest.

Here, outdoor activities – mountain- and quad-biking, hiking, paragliding, fishing and rafting – rival the beauty of the landscapes as the main visitor attractions.

ABOVE The Long Tom Pass winds its way down the Escarpment between Sabie and Lydenberg. En route it cuts through some of the largest man-made forests in the world.

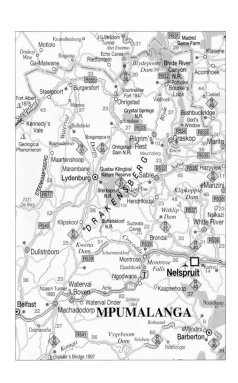

ABOVE A street scene in Sabie, located at the base of Mount Anderson.

Among the region's excellent hikes are the 'Big 5' trails – the Prospector's and Fortune-seeker's Trail is one such – which all take five days or longer, together with a number of shorter, usually three- or four-day routes.

Heading out of Sabie towards Lydenburg leads you up the beautiful, winding Long Tom Pass, named after the huge 50 mm field gun used by the retreating Boers during the Anglo-Boer War (1899–1902); a replica of the cannon marks the site of the engagement.

So good are the roads in this grandly scenic area that many people bring or hire motorbikes to explore it.

GRASKOP

Most visitors explore the Escarpment region on self-drive excursions, but there are two other, really excellent ways to enjoy the splendid countryside. One is by motorbike, and the other is from the air. For the latter, a small helicopter is probably the ideal option.

The 'Fabulous Falls' flight, which leaves from Hazyview on the Lowveld some way to the east (see p. 14), and flies over the Lisbon Falls, the Berlin Falls and then, the most dramatic section, along the edge of the Escarpment, from which the most spectacular views of The Pinnacle and the forests unfold. Another, slightly longer flight will take you over Mac-Mac Falls and Pools, along the Escarpment to Kowyns Pass (which is outside Graskop), and over the Graskop Gorge.

The most visually memorable flight, however, is the 30-minute one that brings you right into the Blyde River Canyon, over its Three Rondavels massifs and the Blyde Dam. The return trip includes a view of the Bourke's Luck Potholes (an eye-catching collection of weirdly eroded rocks; see further on) and then follows the edge of the Escarpment over God's Window and the Berlin and Lisbon falls. The pilots are pretty flexible and will vary the flight route to suit personal preferences.

The Maria Shires is just one of the many falls found in the upland region.

A WONDERLAND OF WATERFALLS

Within the small area bounded by Lydenburg, Sabie, Graskop and the Blyde River Canyon are some of the most dramatic waterfalls and beautiful scenic spots in the entire region.

Near the entrance bridge outside Sabie (off the R532 on the old Lydenburg road) are the Bridal Falls, Lone Creek Falls and Horseshoe Falls. Entrance is through the forest reserve. You may be asked to pay a token fee at the forestry checkpoint.

Heading north from Sabie towards Graskop on the R532 are the Forest Falls, Mac-Mac Falls and the Mac-Mac Pools and, on the opposite side of the road, the smaller Maria Shires Falls. Although Maria Shires is not one of the region's bigger or more dramatic cascades, it certainly has claim to be one of the prettiest, tucked away as it is in the deep-green depths of the forest. At the base of the falls there is a lovely, cool picnic spot, a wooden bench and a little boardwalk set under the trees. A muddy path winds up the hill behind the waterfall to a small graveyard where Maria Shires, a long-gone local lady, rests in peace.

Lisbon Falls and Berlin Falls (each just over 30 metres high) can be reached off the R532 that leads out of Graskop.

Just outside Graskop, still on the R532, you can park your car and take a short walk through the indigenous shrubs to the God's Window and Wonderview sites, well-signposted wooden platforms that offer the most stunning vistas over the Escarpment. Here the land drops away almost vertically to the Lowveld, and standing at God's Window, at an altitude of around two kilometres, leaves you feeling as if you are, literally, on top of the world.

Just before God's Window is The Pinnacle, a massive freestanding quartzite rock that towers above the indigenous forest. From the viewsite just below, eight waterfalls plunge down in a series of alternating sheer drops and cascades. Unfortunately, however, much of this can only be viewed properly from the air.

The Lone Creek Falls, a premier mountain-biking spot.

If helicopter flights are not exciting enough for you, you can float above this magnificent segment of Africa in a hot-air balloon with Balloons Over Africa. Weather permitting, flights generally leave from either White River or Hazyview. The experience is one that will linger in the memory long after you leave this entrancing land: you waft gently over waterfalls and peer over the Escarpment down onto the Lowveld as it stretches across the horizon towards the Kruger Park. The chief pilot has been the South African hot-air ballooning champion on six occasions so you can relax and enjoy the trip knowing you'll be absolutely safe in his experienced hands.

PILGRIM'S REST

Pigrim's Rest is a delightful if somewhat tourist-orientated village, the only one in the country to have been declared a national monument in its entirety. It began life as a lively mining settlement that made its appearance almost overnight after the discovery of alluvial gold in the surrounding hills. In its heyday, it accommodated about 1 600 diggers. Restored wood-and-iron miners' cottages, some of which have been converted into shops, restaurants and coffee houses, line each side of the main road. The village also offers six museums and numerous art and craft galleries.

The well-preserved Victorian-era Royal Hotel charmingly recreates the way

of life enjoyed, and often exuberantly celebrated, in the latter part of the 19th and early 20th centuries. Many of its rooms are in the 39 period cottages adjacent to the main building. The hotel bar was once a school chapel in Cape Town, and was shipped wholesale to the Mozambican port of Delagoa Bay (now Maputo) and later transported, by ox-wagon, over the rugged, fever-ridden lowland plains and up the high Escarpment to Pilgrim's Rest.

Features of the Digging-site Museum, about two kilometres out of town, include prospectors' tents, a jail tent (complete with stocks), wattle-and-daub huts, and a few other buildings. Here you can also see demonstrations of gold-panning beside the nearby creek, from where the gold was originally extracted (and, for good measure, poke around in the water with a pan in search of traces of the yellow metal – an appealing little treasure-hunt). The enjoyable tours are led by a local guide, and take about an hour to complete.

Two other must-see places to visit in the Pilgrim's Rest area are Alanglade House, which represents the more affluent side of the early gold-mining industry, and the small, historic cemetery up on the hill above the village. Alanglade, situated a few kilometres north of town, was built in 1915 as the mine manager's official residence, and is furnished with pieces dating from 1900 to 1930. A visit to the cemetery is also fascinating,

TOP Historic Pilgrim's Rest nestles among once gold-rich hills.
ABOVE One of the town's many wood-and-iron miners' cottages.
BELOW Enthusiasts still pan for gold in the streams around Pilgrim's Rest.

ABOVE The magnificent king cheetah, one of the icons of the Mpumalanga bush, is successfully bred at the Hoedspruit Research and Breeding Centre for Endangered Species.
BELOW Ndebele women in traditional garb sell their wares outside a small craft shop in Pilgrim's Rest.

evoking all the dangers and hardships of life in this little boom town at the turn of the century. Of the 320 known graves, only 163 are marked with headstones. The cosmopolitan character of the gold fields is reflected in the many different nationalities of the people buried here. Accident and disease – drowning, snake bite, pneumonia, dysentery and so forth – were the main causes of death, and struck at the diggers' families as well as at the miners themselves: a number of graves are those of children.

HAZYVIEW
Shangana Cultural Village
Shangana village is situated near Hazyview on the R535 from Graskop.

Tours around this traditional village offer an intriguing insight into the history of the Shangaan people, their culture and their traditions.

The Shangaan are traditionally great farmers, and the tour, appropriately, winds through their small fields and the surrounding bush. Your guide will tell you, among much else, which of the crops are edible, and which are used for traditional medicine. Demonstrations of the time-honoured farming methods are laid on, and villagers will sometimes dress in *masocho* (warrior) garb or other traditional clothing.

Craftsmen from the village and the surrounding areas work and trade in the marketplace at the entrance to the village,

where you can buy anything from clay pots to contemporary metalwork.

On the midday tour, visitors share a meal comprising an array of dishes made from local produce, fresh from the fields and served in wooden pots, bowls and on plates. Among the more memorable menu items is a serving of wonderful, high-protein mopane worms!

But the best tours are arguably those held in the evening, which offer entertainment at its traditional best. The drums start up and a torch-led procession arrives in the large boma area, after which choirs sing, people dance and tell stories, and a feast is served around the massive central bonfire.

Kapama Private Game Reserve
Located on the main R40 road, between Hazyview and the East Gate Airport at Hoedspruit, is Kapama Private Game Reserve, a 12 000-hectare expanse of beautiful bushveld and natural home to Africa's 'big five' (lion, leopard, elephant, rhino, buffalo). Kapama also conserves a multitude of other game, together with a myriad birds and indigenous plant species.

The main camp, Kapama Lodge, is set on a tranquil lake in the centre of the reserve with sweeping views across bushveld and water. There is a wonderful 'tea deck' from where you can watch the water birds. The smaller Buffalo Camp has an East African safari theme, with luxury tents set high on stilts so you feel as if you're sleeping in the tree-tops. The third accommodation option is attractive Nyala Guest House.

Game drives are run from all the camps, and are available to visitors even if they are not staying over. So too are the reserve's gourmet barbecues.

One of Kapama's main drawcards is the Hoedspruit Research and Breeding Centre for Endangered Species, which was established in 1990. The Hoedspruit Safari Park is part of the centre, which runs a large-scale and most successful cheetah breeding programme. At the time of writing, it held more than 60 of these beautiful big cats.

Part of the Safari Park tour takes in a visit to the pens to view the cheetah cubs – and to stroke some of the adults (under the watchful eye of a guide). Here too

you'll see the rare king cheetah (a genetic variant rather than a different species, but majestic nonetheless) for which the park is famous.

The research and breeding programme includes a variety of other rare, endangered, exotic or otherwise interesting species, some of which will be either sold to other reserves or reintroduced into the wild. Tours are conducted in a mini-bus: even though this is very much a 'safari park', its visitor routines are extremely well organised, and they offer you the opportunity to view and enjoy animals that you may never see in the wild – or anywhere else for that matter. For instance, it's estimated there are fewer than six Barbary (North African) lions left in the world, and two of them, rescued from captivity in appalling conditions, have a home at the centre. Other stopovers on the tour take in lions, rhino, buffalo and the endangered Cape hunting dog, or wild dog, long treated by farmers as vermin, belatedly recognised as a uniquely social species and now being pulled back from the brink of extinction. There's also an excellent veterinary hospital that looks after injured or destitute animals.

Moholoholo

Moholoholo, situated on the R531 about 14 kilometres from Klaserie, is another of the Lowveld's wildlife rehabilitation centres. The name means 'The Very Great One', and refers to the big backdrop mountain at the foot of which nestles the centre's Forest Camp, its Mountain View cottages and its lovely tea garden.

Visitors to the centre are introduced to a raptor display that includes several injured or abandoned birds of prey that have been rescued, and some of them are remarkably tame. It's quite a thrill, if somewhat disconcerting, when the vultures come pecking at your shoelaces as you walk around! Other pens house seldom-seen cervals, which are bred at the centre, and a number of other, smaller cats. Among the drawcards are the lions, mostly rescued circus animals living out their well-earned retirement in a large enclosure. One can also visit the small animal clinic. Forest Camp consists of comfortable log-and-thatch cabins set

among the trees; a short walk away is the main dining area, with its open viewing terrace looking out onto the forest. At night bush-pigs will arrive to snuffle around in the undergrowth. During the day, the forest animals – antelope and monkeys among them – patronise the water hole.

The bigger Mountain View Camp has self-catering cottages as well as dormitory accommodation. The latter also caters for school groups and other parties of people interested in wildlife education or game-ranger courses. The wildlife education trails are fun as well as instructive: among other things, you get to study animal spoor and learn some basic tree and bird identification.

The nearby Ya Miti tea garden is set right alongside a bubbling river in a large grassy patch under massive shady trees. There's also a pretty little stone chapel, which is used for weddings and other functions.

Bombyx Mori Silk Farm

Silk production is generally associated with China and other Far Eastern countries. However, just 20 minutes from Hoedspruit's East Gate Airport, along the R531, is an unusual farm that produces high-quality silk.

A tour through Bombyx Mori begins with an audio-visual presentation and an introduction, both to the farm and to silk farming in Africa, before heading out to the silkworm hatchery. The eggs are

ABOVE The Escarpment viewed from the bird hide at Moholoholo Rehabilitation Centre near Hoedspruit.
BELOW The Moholoholo camp nestles in the depths of indigenous forest.
BOTTOM Thrills and spills on the Sabie River as rafters challenge the white waters.

TOP *A stunning view of the Three*
Rondavels from a vantage point overlooking
the Blyde River Canyon.
ABOVE *Water, sand and pebbles have*
scoured the strange rock formations known
as the Bourke's Luck Potholes.
BELOW *Silkworms spin their cocoons*
in special trays, to produce fabric for
duvets and other products, at the Bombyx
Mori farm.

viewed through a small window – one
can't actually enter because strictly
controlled conditions are needed to keep
the temperature constant and diseases
and infection at bay. This is followed by a
tour of the 'eating shed', where millions
of silkworms spend their days munching
on fresh mulberry leaves harvested each
morning on the surrounding farm. A
number of local women are employed as
trained skilled silk weavers, harvesting
the silk by hand and processing it into
attractive duvets, cushions, pillows,
garments and other handspun products.

BLYDE RIVER CANYON

The Blyde River ('river of joy') refers to
a happy reunion that took place among
a Voortrekker party in the early 1840s:
a group of men who had set off in an
attempt to find a route to the coast, were
late in returning (and given up for dead)
but eventually did so and arrived back to
an ecstatic welcome. The water tumbles
through a deep and spectacular gorge,
part of which is dammed, most of which
runs through the Blyde River Nature
Reserve. There are a number of
wonderful viewsites from which to enjoy
the dramatic canyon with its towering red
and gold sandstone cliffs.

The Three Rondavels, gigantic
formations that are also known as The

Chief's Wives, dominate the northern
section of the canyon. Two high bridges
across the gorge offer grand views of the
Bourke's Luck Potholes, a moonscape of
deep hollows and channels near the
confluence of the Blyde and Treur rivers.

The Potholes, some of them six metres
deep, have been formed over centuries of
continuous scouring by sand and pebbles
carried along by the river. Not far away is
the headquarters of the Blyde River
Nature Reserve – which looks out over
the Blydepoort Dam – and the visitors'
centre, from where you can see the
attractive Kadishi waterfall.

The pleasant and popular Blyde
River Canyon Hiking Trail leads from
Paradise Camp to Waterval Spruit about
3 kilometres away, then on to Clearstream,
a further 13.5 kilometres, and to the old
mining hut at Bourke's Luck Potholes.

Approximately 16 kilometres to the
north of the village of Bourke's Luck is
the popular Aventura Swadini, a large
resort that has been renamed a number
of times over the years but remains a
well-run, popular family holiday
destination that offers a number of
activities from boating to hiking. Here
there's a restaurant and a swimming pool,
and accommodation in chalets.

A variety of games are organised
throughout the holiday months and
other busy periods; out of season, the
atmosphere at the dam and canyon is
a little less frenetic.

A number of tour operators run
rafting trips through the canyon.

Swadini Reptile Park

The exterior of the park is rather
ordinary, perhaps, but inside you'll find
quite an impressive variety of reptiles
ranging from crocodiles to leguaans. The
biggest attraction, though, is the circular
route that makes its way around the
glassed-in snake enclosures. Housed
within them are long, sparkly-eyed green
mambas, wicked-looking but magnificent
black mambas, puff adders, pythons and
a number of other indigenous snakes,
together with exotic species from places
as far afield as South America.

Monsoon Crafts

About halfway between Swadini Reptile
Park (on the R527) and the turnoff onto

the R36 and the Strijdom Tunnel, is Monsoon Crafts. You'll find parking just off the main road. The complex in the parking area has a wonderful restaurant – Mad Dogz – which serves light meals and refreshments, and an excellent craft shop that sells both local and other African crafts. This is a great place to stop and rest during a long, hot journey. Attached to the restaurant is another small shop stocked with products from the Bombyx Mori Silk Farm (see p. 15).

MOUNT ANDERSON

Some of the finest trout fishing in the country can be enjoyed within the rough triangle bounded by Lydenburg, Dullstroom and Machadadorp. Much of it is confined by dams, but there's also fine sport to be had along the banks of the area's many lovely rivers and streams. Set high on the 2 284-metre Mount Anderson, outside the substantial town of Lydenburg, is one of the country's premier trout-fishing lodges, a standing credit to the Rattray family (who also own the well-known Mala Mala reserve).

To stay at the Mount Anderson lodge is fairly expensive, but the accommodation, food and service are all geared to the top end of the market, and the surrounding countryside is quite magnificent. Golden Cottage offers three luxurious suites; the main homestead houses the dining room, fully equipped modern kitchen, comfy TV lounge with a big fireplace, and a

magnificent sun-room with a stunning view over the trout dams and the valley beyond. A number of indigenous wild animals, mainly antelope, live on the estate, and high on the cliffs behind the house is a vulture colony.

Guests may explore the estate on horseback; points of interest en route include the ruins of centuries-old mines; the scenery is superb.

Even if you're not an experienced fly-fisherman, it is almost impossible not to catch a trout in one of the well-stocked, stepped dams that tier down from the front of the lodge.

Dullstroom and Machadadorp

Dullstroom is set at the edge of the lofty Steenkampsberg range, about 60 kilometres on the R540 from Lydenburg. Nestled on the slopes of the 2 300-metre Groot Suikerboschkop, it's the province's highest town, a charming little centre reminiscent of a Scottish village. Many of the houses are old – the town dates back to 1883 – and are built of stone. The village, occupied and virtually destroyed by the British during the Anglo-Boer War, has long since been resurrected to become the attractive hub of the country's most popular trout-fishing region.

There are two excellent dams on the Crocodile River, where anglers fly-fish for both brown and rainbow trout.

ABOVE The Blyde River winds its way through the mountains of the Escarpment and into the Blydepoort Dam, a popular recreation area.
BOTTOM LEFT The boomslang ranks among the most venomous of South Africa's snakes but, despite its prevalence in the area, is seldom seen.
BELOW The malachite kingfisher is glimpsed as a flash of blue as the tiny bird moves from perch to riverside perch.

17

TOP AND ABOVE Some of the finest trout fishing in the country can be enjoyed in the clear mountain waters of the Dullstroom-Lydenburg area.
BELOW Mount Anderson Lodge is one of the most exclusive of the region's fly-fishing venues, with the trout-stocked waters, literally, on its doorstep.

Permits for fly-fishing can be obtained from shops in the village. The small Verlorenvallei Nature Reserve, close to town, is the only protected place in South Africa where all three crane species – blue, wattled and crowned – can be seen.

Machadadorp is also an angling centre, but is just as popular among hikers and bird-watchers. Most of the guest farms and lodges around the little town have one or more private dams for fly-fishing; many allow the use of float tubes and kick boats, offer tuition, and hire out fly-fishing equipment.

WATERVAL-BOVEN AND WATERVAL-ONDER

These villages are – much as their names imply – twinned, one set above the Elands Falls waterfall and one below. Both are popular fly-fishing venues.

Waterval-Onder comprises little more than a small hotel and a station. A steam train runs between the two centres each Sunday, stopping off at the waterfall and other picturesque spots along the way. Also on the linking line is the old rail tunnel, 400 metres long, through which guided tours are taken. The tunnel was completed in 1884, but fell into disuse in 1904.

Although this area may seem rather insignificant on the map, it is in fact visually enchanting and popular among hikers. The rocky cliffs around the village also provide some good rock-climbing and paragliding venues.

SUDWALA CAVES AND DINOSAUR PARK

Between Waterval-Onder and Nelspruit are some of the oldest caves in the world. Pass through their main entrance, which is in the forest that flanks the Mankelekele ('High-on-High') mountain, and you'll find yourself in an amazing labyrinth that takes you down into the bowels of the earth. It is believed that the caverns were formed over a period of more than a million years, during which water seeped slowly through the rock and dissolved the dolomite. The wonderful dripstone formations have such evocative, and descriptive names as the Screaming Monster, the Weeping Madonna, Nick the Devil, Samson's Pillar and the Rocket Silo. Embedded in the roof of one of the caves are collenia, strange, saucer-like depressions of fossilised colonies of blue-green algae that were thought to have lived, if that's the right word, some 2 000 million years ago. These fossils can also be seen in the vast, echoing cavern known as the PR Owen Chamber.

Tours of the caves last for about an hour and a half. Longer excursions into the deeper recesses can be arranged in advance.

Nearby is the Dinosaur Park, with its extraordinary sculptures and models of some of the fearsome creatures that roamed the earth millions of years ago. The models are scattered throughout the park, among indigenous trees and ancient cycads. One life-sized *Tyrannosaurus rex* towers six metres into the sky; a mighty *Diplodocus* stands knee-deep in a large pond; about a hundred other extinct creatures can be seen on the short circular paths that wind through park. In another section there's a series of six sculptures depicting the evolution of the horse family, *Equus*.

The only live 'dinosaurs' to be seen are the crocodiles lazing in a pit near the end of the walkway.

BARBERTON
Eureka City Ghost Town Tours
In the late 1800s, when hordes of fortune-seekers travelled across the subcontinent in the hope of finding gold, the world's richest deposit of the precious yellow metal was discovered in the

'Golden Quarry' in the hills above the town of Barberton.

Yielding some 109 grams of gold per ton of rock excavated (compared with the Witwatersrand's best yield of 10 grams per ton), the Golden Quarry was indeed a gold-digger's paradise.

Around the quarry grew Eureka City, a remarkably lively mining centre in which the population, by 1887, numbered some 700, and which boasted stores, pubs, hotels, a post office and even a racecourse.

Today, all that is left of Eureka City are a few sun-bleached ruins hidden away in the long grass.

Visitors can tour the ruins and the quarry, an awesome, man-made cavern with massive pillars holding up the tunnels and chambers of the once rich workings. This 'cave' is considered one of the wonders of the mining world. On the way up the mountain, which is negotiated in a four-wheel-drive vehicle, you see some of the oldest rock formations on earth, fossils of blue-green algae (thought to have been the earliest form of life on earth), and a 3 500-million-year-old fossilised beach.

ABOVE: Barberton, once a big and busy mining centre, now a sleepy little town set beneath the 'Golden Quarry'.

No visit to Pilgrim's Rest would be complete without a drink at the historic Royal Hotel.

Prince
of Parks

Kruger National Park

*T*he Kruger National Park ranks among the world's great
game sanctuaries, and serves as one of South Africa's
premier tourist destinations. Covering nearly 20 000 square
kilometres (which is about the size of Wales), it is haven to
a vast array of wildlife, including more than 140 species of
mammal. Among the latter are the famed 'big five' of the
African veld. The park's many rest camps are oases in a
magnificent wilderness; it has a well-developed network
of roads, and it offers the ultimate in terms of both
game-viewing and family comfort.

Kruger National Park

The Kruger, MalaMala Private Game Reserve

Well-developed air and good road links connect the Johannebsurg–Pretoria area with the Kruger. The main highway east is the N4, which leads directly from Pretoria to and beyond Nelspruit, the region's main town. From Johannesburg, take the R22 and then join the N4 near Witbank.

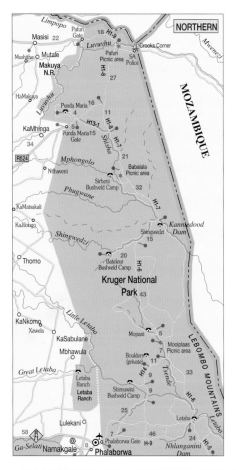

THE KRUGER STORY

From relatively humble beginnings, the Kruger National Park has become one of the jewels in the southern African tourism crown, hosting more than 5 000 well-satisfied visitors a day.

The vast, heat-hazed lowland plain which the park now occupies (in part) has always been big-game country, but with the coming of the white settlers it became a hunter's paradise, and by the end of the 19th century many mammal species were in grave danger of regional extinction. The slaughter, the destruction of the country's great natural heritage, deeply distressed the Transvaal's (or more correctly the Zuid-Afrikaansche Republiek's) old president, Paul Kruger, who eventually managed to elevate a modest 4 600 square kilometres to the status of a game protection area, which was named the Sabie Game Reserve. A year later, an expanse of bushveld to the north of the Letaba River was also proclaimed, and was named the Shingwedzi Game Reserve. The Sabie and Shingwedzi reserves were then joined to form what is known today as the Kruger National Park. The Kruger was opened to the public as a tourist venue on 31 May 1926 – Africa's first official wilderness, and still among its biggest and best known. Today, it stretches for 350 kilometres from the Crocodile River in the south, along the Mozambique border to the confluence of the Limpopo and Levuvhu rivers in the north, the point where the South African, Mozambican and Zimbabwean borders meet.

THE PARK

The Kruger National Park is home to numerous indigenous African bird, insect, reptile and mammal species, including the 'big five', namely lion, leopard, elephant, rhino and buffalo. The presence of these charismatic animals, together with the opportunity to see antelope of many kinds, giraffe, hippopotamus and large herds of wildebeest, all in their natural surroundings, is the principal drawcard. However, it is not just the large and sometimes dangerous life forms that have appeal. There are close to 150 mammal species, over 380 species of indigenous tree, 45 species of lizard, 34 different amphibians and more than 500 species of bird. In fact, many people visit the park just to see the birds, spending hours sitting quietly at the many beautiful water holes with their bird books and binoculars. Others visit at different times of the year, enjoying the seasonal changes in the environment, periods when the various shrubs and trees come into flower or drop their leaves, or when the water dries up and the grass changes from summer green to winter blonde.

The park can be divided roughly into three regions – the south, central and northern, each with something different to offer. There are about 3 000 kilometres of good roads, and plenty for the visitor to see and do.

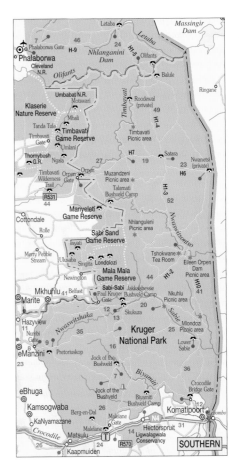

ENJOYING THE KRUGER

The following few suggestions are worth bearing in mind – they are intended to help you make your stay in the Kruger more enjoyable.

School holidays are usually very busy, especially in the southern and central regions of the park, so if you plan to visit at these times, book well in advance.

Opinions differ about the best season in which to tour the Kruger. Some feel that the winter months are the optimum for viewing game because the grass is short, the trees leafless (so spotting game becomes easier) and the animals also tend to congregate around water holes. However, the wildlife is still visible in the moist summer months, and you'll see them in healthier condition. It's also a time of regeneration, when the newborn are experiencing their days of wonder. Moreover, the summertime countryside is green and pleasant, the trees and shrubs (many of them) in flower, the rivers full, the migrant birds in residence.

Kruger can get exceptionally hot during the summer months so, if that is your choice, plan your game drives for the early mornings and late evenings – which are in any case the best game-viewing hours. Many of the rest camps have swimming pools, and you'll be able to cool off during the heat of the day. Pack sun-protection gear – suntan lotion, sunglasses, wide-brimmed hat. Winter nights can get really cold; you'll need warm clothing, especially for the early morning and night drives.

The park is also a high-risk malaria area, but this shouldn't be a problem. Just take the standard precautions. Check with your doctor, pharmacist or travel clinic about the malaria prophylactic you should be using and follow the instructions to the letter. Invest in a good insect repellent (there are a number on the market). Wear cool, long-sleeved shirts and long trousers with shoes and socks, particularly in the evenings and early mornings when you are most likely to be bitten by mosquitoes. At night, sleep under a mosquito net.

Day Drives

Although you can arrange to be driven around by a private operator, or on an organised National Parks game excursion, most visitors choose the self-drive option. Maps are available from camp offices. It's also a good idea to check the camp's game notice boards for recent sightings – many animals are territorial and don't always move over long distances, so there is a chance that you will be able to find them in the same vicinity. Also, check with the camp warden about the hides and water holes near your camp. When you've chosen a route to follow, leave as early as possible in the morning. You aren't allowed outside camp at night.

Drive really slowly. The speed limits are 50 km/h on tar and 40 on gravel, but

ABOVE The Zulu people call the giraffe iNdlulamiti, *which means 'the one that passes the trees'.*
OPPOSITE Elephant cows are highly protective of their young.
TOP LEFT The turkey-sized ground hornbill, and the mighty lion.
PREVIOUS PAGES Arguably Africa's most elusive cat, the beautifully camouflaged leopard is known as the 'prince of stealth'.

TOP, ABOVE AND BELOW A Kruger dam (the Rooibosrand) at sunset; night game-drive; saddle-billed stork.

you should actually travel at a much more leisurely rate than this if you're to get the most out of the tour. The slow crawl makes spotting game a lot easier and gives you time to notice the smaller things: a snake sunning itself on the road, for example; or a tree in flower, or a rare bird half hidden in the foliage – things you'll never notice if you speed by.

You are only allowed to get out of your car at designated viewing spots, picnic sites and some of the monuments, so pack refreshments for your drive. And do not, ever, get out of your car in an area that is not so designated – the Kruger is a well-organised tourism venue, but it's also wild Africa.

Some of the most popular and productive game-viewing can be enjoyed in the park's southern region, in a rough triangle formed by the roads between Skukuza, Lower Sabie and Tshokwane picnic site.

Night Drives

You may not, as mentioned, drive yourself around the park at night, but you can go out after dark on a ranger-led drive – a very special experience, when you see nocturnal animals that are otherwise elusive.

Rangers use powerful spotlights from open vehicles to focus on such minor characters as bushbabies (galagos), porcupines, servals, civets, owls, nightjars, the weird dikkops and other night birds. If you're lucky, you could also spot big cats – lions and leopards – and hyenas on the hunt. Put on warm gear when the sun goes down (it can become very chilly on the back of the vehicle). And remember to take a torch. Drives may be booked through the camp office.

Hides and Water Holes

Those who prefer not to spend their days driving can choose to spend time at a few good water holes and hides not too far from camp. Some spots are better during a particular season, so check beforehand with your camp warden. Remember to pack your field guides and binoculars, and be prepared to be patient, and quiet. Sometimes you have to wait a while for interesting animals to make their way down to the water hole, but you can always occupy the time by looking out for, and identifying, the birds. Or just enjoy the tranquillity.

Wilderness Trails

For many people, this is the ultimate wilderness experience. You have a choice of seven trails, and none of them demands special physical fitness. But you do need to be able to walk (slowly) some 18 kilometres in a day.

An armed ranger leads a group of up to eight people through the bush on foot, returning to the trail camp each night. The trail camps are rustic affairs with reed-walled showers and toilets. Meals are simple but hearty, and are usually enjoyed around a campfire.

The idea behind the wilderness trails is to experience, and enjoy, nature at its most immediate and intimate, and many trailists report thrilling close encounters with wild animals – even with rhino, elephant and lion. However, it is perhaps more fun (and less heart-stopping) to learn about the ecology of the region and some of the basic bush skills – how to recognise animal tracks, medicinal trees, various birds and so forth.

The seven wilderness trails are: the Bushman, which takes its name from the ancient rock art found in the region; the Metsimetsi, (*metsi* is an African name for water, which refers to the nearby

SAFARI IN STYLE

Along and near the Kruger park's western, open boundary you'll find some splendid private game reserves, most of them offering the ultimate in safari comfort and the best of game-viewing experiences. Mala Mala is among the finest, and is perhaps the best known internationally. Set in the magnificent Sabi Sands area, it comprises three luxurious camps on 18 000 hectares of pristine wilderness.

The reserve shares a 26-kilometre border with the Kruger, occupying an area known to have the greatest diversity of animal species on the African continent. Over 200 different mammals occur here in great numbers, and the bird life is outstanding. Game continually crosses unhindered between Mala Mala and Kruger. The habitat includes open grassland and rocky outcrops, thick riverine forest and acacia and combretum bushveld. The Sand River flows north-south through the reserve for 45 kilometres. Mala Mala's three camps are Main, Harry's and Kirkman's, each with its own design, decor and character. Service is personalised and outstanding (all the camp's rangers have university degrees in the natural sciences). Game drives are rated among the best in the country.

On arrival you are assigned a ranger who, from then on, looks after you, makes sure that you have everything you need and, helped by a local tracker, takes you on morning and evening drives, and, on request, on walks through the bush. Most of the trackers have years of experience behind them, highly tuned senses, and an intimate knowledge of the bush. A recorded 76 per cent of guests have contact sightings of the 'big five'.

Over the years, Mala Mala has been awarded many honours. In 2001, *Travel and Leisure* Magazine ranked it first in the category 'World's Best Service for Africa and the Middle East'.

N'waswitsontso River); the Napi, well known for its white rhino sightings; the really remote Nyalaland Trail in the far north (excellent bird-watching opportunities); the Wolhuter, which runs mid-way between Pretoriuskop and Berg-en-Dal (also good for white rhino); the Olifants, which winds through both riverine forest and the rocky foothills of the Lebombo Mountains, and lastly the Sweni Trail, east of Satara.

THE REST CAMPS

The choice of accommodation is varied, ranging from places that are more like busy little villages than safari venues down to tented camps in the wilderness, and from fairly rustic huts and self-catering chalets to luxuriously appointed guesthouses. Even though the main rest camps offer standard facilities, such as petrol outlets, restaurants and shops selling basic commodities, each has its own character and special features, and prices vary accordingly. Booking in advance may be necessary for many of the camps, especially during peak season.

Balule

Situated in the central region, on the banks of the Olifants River about 87 kilometres from the Phalaborwa Gate, Balule is a fairly small camp, with a site for tents and caravans as well as rustic accommodation. However, many people enjoy the place for its 'back-to-nature' feel – there is no shop, and no electricity, just lamps and coal stoves. The bathrooms and cooking facilities all operate on a communal basis.

Berg-en-Dal

Located in the Kruger's southern region, this is one of the larger camps, offering neat self-catering chalets, camping and caravaning sites, an air-conditioned

ABOVE Leopard cubs seem to have an inborn hunting ability, and leave their mother to make their own way in the bush when they are about 18 months old. BELOW Newborn buffalo calves are particularly vulnerable to predation, especially by lions, even though they manage to walk within minutes of birth.

TOP *Giraffe are inquisitive creatures and will often peer curiously at you from their great height.*
ABOVE *Among the shyest of the antelope, the kudu is also one of the largest. Males bear a magnificent set of spiralled horns; females are hornless.*

restaurant, pool, coin laundry, fast-food outlet, a well-stocked store and an open-air theatre where wildlife films are sometimes shown. The chalets are strategically set among some lovely indigenous riverine vegetation, providing more privacy than found at some of the other camps. The small Matjulu Dam, situated near the perimeter fence, is surrounded by a paved walkway and is a fine spot for observing the game, the birds and, most especially, the crocodiles. Berg-en-Dal's night drives are popular, and should be booked in advance. The camp is known for its sightings of wild dog, white rhino and leopard.

Crocodile Bridge

The camp is located in the far southeastern corner of the Park, about 13 kilometres from Komatipoort and, as the name suggests, on the bank of the Crocodile River. The venue is fairly small, popular as a one- or two-night stopover before venturing further into the

park. It is also near the Crocodile Bridge Gate, which is a bit of a drawback during peak season, when the through traffic is considerable. On the downside, too, is the vista – from here you can see the commercial farms and some power-lines on the southern bank of the river. However, the camp itself is attractive and shady, the accommodation comfortable and the game-viewing in the vicinity highly rated. The camp has a shop, laundromat and petrol station.

Letaba

This is a large camp about 50 kilometres from the Phalaborwa Gate in the central region of the park – an area recognised as prime elephant country. Its huts are thatched, the surrounding grounds full of apple-leaf and acacia trees. There is also a shady campground on the perimeter fence. The restaurant's outdoor seating affords a fine view over the broad, sandy riverbed in the Letaba valley. The Engelhardt and Mingerhout are two

nearby dams that attract elephant and a variety of other general game species.

Letaba is also in the centre of what are considered to be three of the most popular and productive of the game drives – two lead to Satara and Olifants in the south, the third goes up towards Shingwedzi in the north. The Elephant Hall Museum, situated inside Letaba's Goldfields Environmental Centre, is worth a visit – it tells a comprehensive story of the animal, its physical nature, its social behaviour and of the work carried out by the Endangered Species Protection Unit, a special police task force dedicated to protecting wild animals against illegal trade and poaching. Here too there is an interesting exhibition display featuring six of the Kruger's legendary 'Magnificent Seven' tuskers, whose ivory is on display.

Like many of the larger camps, Letaba has a petrol station, a shop and cafeteria (take-aways), a laundromat and information centre.

Lower Sabie

The Lower Sabie Rest Camp in southern Kruger, about 35 kilometres north of Crocodile Bridge, is an ideal base for game drives and popular among families. It has beautiful lawns, big shady trees and lovely views of the Sabie River. The area around the camp is mainly grassland savanna dotted with marula and knobthorn trees and offers excellent game-viewing – hippo, crocodiles and an interesting variety of birds – at a number of nearby watering places, among them the Sunset and the Lower Sabie dams. A little further north is the Mlondozi Dam, which has a pretty picnic site. The Lower Sabie camp has its own petrol station, laundromat, restaurant, self-service and take-away cafeteria and shop.

Mopani

This large camp, in the north-central region about 70 kilometres northeast of Phalaborwa Gate, is one of the Kruger's newest. Situated at the foot of a rocky

ABOVE Impala lambs are born in November, virtually en masse to confuse predators. They soon form nurseries, where they groom each other with specially adapted teeth.
BELOW A relative of the ground hornbill, the yellow-billed hornbill's distinctive 'tok tok tok' call makes it easy to locate.

coming down to the river to drink. An excellent game-viewing drive is that along the course of the Olifants and nearby Letaba rivers.

Olifants has a restaurant, petrol station, shop, laundromat and take-away cafeteria, but no camping facilities.

Pretoriuskop

This large rest camp, just 9 kilometres from the Numbi Gate in the park's southwestern region, features lovely shade trees and an attractive plant life, though perhaps it falls a little short on privacy. Be that as it may, there is much to see in the area. The Albasini Ruins are not far away and the Hippo Pool/Doispane road offers stunning views of the Sabie River. The surrounding landscape includes some steep, rocky ridges and sourveld vegetation, which attracts browsers such as giraffe, large kudu and other antelope. In turn, the buck attract predators such as wild dog and lion. This is also a good area for white rhino.

The drive between the Pretoriuskop and Skukuza rest camps is considered one of the best for game-viewing.

The camp has a swimming pool, restaurant, petrol outlet, and shop.

Punda Maria

The camp is 10 kilometres from the Punda Maria Gate in northern Kruger, close to the Zimbabwean border, and many of those who manage to make it this far welcome its remoteness and tranquillity. The surrounding area is sandveld, which is botanically varied and thus supports a fascinating variety of plant, bird and animal life. Notable birds include the Narina trogon and Arnot's chat.

There is an interesting trail winding through the camp, and three excellent circular game drives.

Satara

Satara, in the central region about 50 kilometres from Orpen Gate, is the Kruger's second largest rest camp. The knobthorn veld of the area provides good grazing for herds of antelope, and the game concentrations are impressive. There are a number of water holes, pans and dams in the vicinity which also offer good game-viewing opportunities; the drive between the camp and Orpen Gate

ABOVE One of the 'big five', the white rhino gets its name from the Dutch word wydt *(meaning 'wide'), a reference to the square shape of the mouth.*
BELOW Baboons can provide visitors with hours of entertainment as they go about their busy daily lives. On no account, however, should they be fed.

outcrop, it is built of stone, wood and thatch and has a fantastic view out over the Pioneer Dam. There are shaded wood walkways between the public areas. It is surrounded by mopane shrubveld and the game-viewing is perhaps not as consistently rewarding as that in the southern regions but, still, there are some excellent opportunities to see the wildlife, often from the camp itself. Elephant and other animals are attracted to the dam; bird-watching is also good.

There is a petrol station, information centre, restaurant, open-air bar (with stunning views), a swimming pool and a laundromat.

Olifants

Olifants, situated in the central region 82 kilometres from Phalaborwa Gate, has arguably the most attractive setting of all the Kruger's camps. It's a large place atop a rocky cliff from which there are magnificent views over the Olifants River and away into the distance. Massive sausage trees, knobbly sycamore figs and a variety of other indigenous trees draw many species of bird to the camp. A shaded observation platform on the edge of the cliffs invites you to sit for hours with binoculars, watching the animals is especially rewarding. Satara has all the necessary facilities, including petrol station, restaurant, shop, and laundromat.

Shingwedzi

Shingwedzi, in the far north of Kruger (although not as far as Punda Maria) has a rather hot, dry camping ground that doesn't offer much shade, but the rest camp itself is attractive enough, surrounded by mopane shrubveld, which attracts elephants. The region is also known for its leopards, which can sometimes be spotted on the drive along the Shingwedzi River. The waters of the river are home to crocodiles and hippos, and the riverine vegetation is good for bird-watching. In fact, you can see a lot of game without actually moving too far from camp: antelope, zebra and even giraffe can often be observed from the perimeter fence. There is a swimming pool, laundromat, petrol station, restaurant, cafeteria and shop.

Skukuza

Biggest of the rest camps, Skukuza functions as the park's headquarters. Indeed the place is large enough to be considered a small town, offering amenities such as a petrol station, post office, bank, grocery shop, restaurants, library, police station and airport. There is even an education centre and two museums (the Campbell Hut and the Selati Rail).

The thornveld around the camp supports plenty of wildlife, the nearby Sabie River attracting hippos, crocodiles and a variety of birds.

Bushveld Camps

These differ somewhat from the Kruger's bigger rest camps: they are smaller, more intimate and generally more attractive, providing a more 'authentic' wilderness experience. Access is restricted to residents only (no day-visitors), and there are fewer facilities – no petrol station, restaurant or shop.

Most of the bushveld camps are situated in the southern and central regions of the park, with the exception of Bateleur, which is about 40 kilometres southwest of Shingwedzi.

The others are: Sirheni, on the banks of the Sirheni Dam about 55 kilometres from Punda Maria; Biyamiti, Jakkalsbessie, Malelane and Jock of the Bushveld in the southern region, and Talamati, Shimuwini, Nwanetsi, Boulders and Roodewal in the central region.

ABOVE Lilac-breasted rollers, invariably seen sitting on a well-exposed perch, are among the more vividly coloured of the Lowveld birds.

Family rondavels at the Kruger's Lower Sabie rest camp.

USEFUL CONTACTS

South African National Parks
Tel: 012 343 1991
Fax: 012 343 0905
reservations@parks-sa.co.za
www.parks-sa.co.za

Kruger National Park
Tel: 013 735 5159
Fax: 013 735 5154
www.parks-sa.co.za

Mpumalanga Tourism Authority
Tel: 013 752 7001
Fax: 013 759 5441
mtanlpsa@cis.co.za
www.mpumalanga.com

Nelspruit Tourism
Tel: 013 755 1988
Fax: 013 755 1350
nelspruit@soft.co.za
www.lowveldinfo.com

Golden Monkey/Big 5 Central Reservations
Tel: 013 737 8191
Fax: 013 737 8384
goldenm@mweb.co.za
www.big5country.com

Mala Mala
Tel: 031 765 2900
Fax: 031 765 3365
reservations@mala mala.com
www.malamala.com

Other Private Game Reserves
LONDOLOZI
Tel: 011 809 4300
information@ccafrica.com
www.ccafrica.com

DJUMA GAME RESERVE
Tel: 013 735 5118
djuma@djuma.co.za
www.djuma.com

INYATI
Tel: 011 880 5950
inyatitl@iafrica.com
www.inyati.co.za

NGALA
Tel: 011 809 4300
information@ccafrica.com
www.ccafrica.com

SABI SABI
Tel: 011 483 3939
com@sabisabi.com
www.sabisabi.com

Tour Companies
DABULA MANGI SAFARIS
Tel: 013 744 7623
Cell: 083 449 0330
Fax: 013 744 7634
dennie@execubush.com

TOUR D'AFRIQUE
Tel: 013 750 1107
Fax: 013 750 1109
tdawr@mweb.co.za
www.tourdafrique.co.za

VULA TOURS
Tel: 013 741 2238
Fax: 013 741 2238
vula@soft.co.za

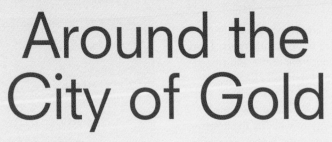

Around the City of Gold

Excursions from Johannesburg

Johannesburg, South Africa's industrial and financial heartland, offers a myriad attractions, not least of them some fine museums (MuseumAfrica is rather special), theatres, grand shopping malls, and a splendid selection of restaurants which, between them, cater for every culinary taste. Gold Reef City, an exuberant re-creation of the early mining days, ranks among the country's top tourist drawcards. The areas within easy driving distance of the central city, however, are also well endowed. These are three suggestions for the visitor who has a day to spare and a mind to spend it exploring.

Excursions from Johannesburg

Soweto, Sterkfontein Cave Complex, Sun City, The Lost City, Pilanesberg National Park.

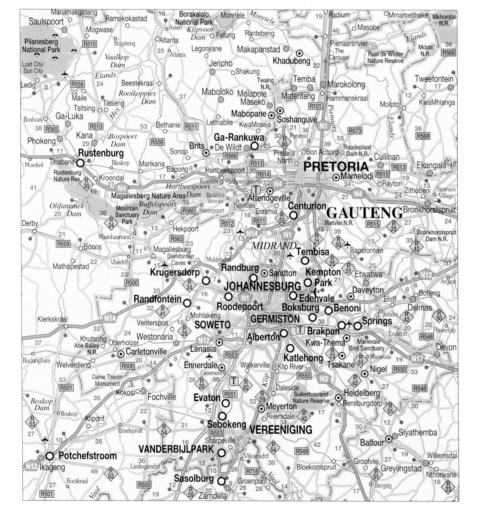

Soweto is an acronym for 'SOuth WEstern TOwnships' and, as the name suggests, it lies just to the southwest of Johannesburg city centre. Not far to the west, around Sterkfontein in the Krugersdorp area, you'll find a series of caves that has a crucial place in the story of early humankind, and beyond, past the lovely Magaliesberg hills and then north on a good road, is Sun City, the first and still the most glamorous of South Africa's inland resorts.

SOWETO TOWNSHIP TOURS

The satellite city (actually, an integral part of the Johannesburg metropolitan complex) is the largest 'township' in Africa. For years it served as the fulcrum of resistance to apartheid, of a sustained and ultimately successful campaign that reached its most dramatic point in 1976, when students rose in revolt against the government, its schooling and language policies and, beyond them, the savagely discriminatory laws of the country.

Today, it is a peaceful, vibrant community, rich in its human diversity. A conducted visit will take in not just the stereotypical town-scapes, though these are interesting enough (they encompass a huge range of lifestyles, from abject, overcrowded poverty to opulence on grand scale) but also many sites of historical significance.

Included will be the Regina Mundi Church, the only 'safe' venue for the many political meetings, protest rallies and community gatherings held during the apartheid years. Inside, you'll see bullet holes in the ceiling and walls, the product of police aggression, and the famous painting of the black Madonna.

Next stop is, usually, the poignant Hector Petersen Memorial, situated in an open square in the suburb of Orlando. Hector, not yet a teenager, was the first child shot and killed by police at the start of the 1976 uprising.

From the memorial, the tour goes to the Orlando West home of Nelson Mandela before he was arrested and sent to prison for 27 years. The house is filled with the original furniture and Mandela family memorabilia.

A number of Soweto tours also include a drive past the one-time home of notables such as Nobel laureate Desmond Tutu, tireless campaigner for human rights. Another route may take you to the Chris Hani-Baragwanath Hospital, the southern hemisphere's largest (the name commemorates, in part, the charismatic struggle hero assassinated by white extremists in 1993), and Avalon Cemetry, resting place of noted political activists such as Helen Joseph and Joe Slovo. Tours invariably end up with drinks or a meal at one of Soweto's celebrated shebeens (taverns).

These conducted trips are quite safe – well organised, led by guides known to the residents. However, it is not a good idea to attempt the visit on your own: street crime remains a factor and, moreover, there are no proper street maps of this massive, sprawling and, to an outsider, confusing area.

STERKFONTEIN CAVES

This complex, to the west of Johannesburg and a proclaimed World Heritage Site, ranks as one of Africa's most important palaeontological sites, with a fossil history that dates back more than three million years. It embraces the Sterkfontein Valley, informally called The Cradle of Man (though the phrase is also applied to Africa as a whole), and the many limestone caves in the surrounding dolomite hills.

In 1947, the Sterkfontein Caves made world headlines when Robert Broom discovered the skull of *Australopithecus africanus*. It belonged to a female hominid who lived in Africa about a million years ago and is known as 'Mrs Ples', after its original scientific name, *Plesianthropus transvaalensis*.

Since then, more than 600 hominid fossils have been discovered in the caves, including the 3.5 million-year-old 'Little Foot' remains in 1994 and the first intact fossilised skeleton of an early ape-man (1998). In April 2000, two more discoveries of great importance were made here: a largely complete skull of a hominid female, and the mandible of a related ape-man, thought to be between one and a half, and two million years old.

A guided tour leaves every hour, taking visitors to an underground lake that has deep significance in local lore. There is a museum complex that offers an insight, expressed in broad terms, into the evolution of humankind.

Wonder Caves, South Africa's third largest, are not far from Sterkfontein, and although they haven't contributed as much to the palaeontological story, they

are visually more dramatic. Like Sterkfontein, they were once mined for their limestone, and comprise some interesting chambers and intriguingly shaped dripstone formations, all of which are floodlit. The entrance is an enormous, 40-metre high cavern. The caves do not have too many visitor facilities, but there's a daily tour.

SUN CITY AND THE LOST CITY

Each year, some two million people visit what is arguably one of the world's most unusual and exciting inland resorts, the unique 'African legend' development of Sun City and The Palace of the Lost City. A 10-minute drive from the complex will take you to Pilanesberg National Park, which sustains the world's third largest white rhino population.

The Sun City complex began as an opulent, man-made fantasy world focused mainly on casino gaming rooms, outdoor water features, beautifully landscaped grounds and a massive 'Superbowl' entertainment centre. In the past 10 years the resort has expanded significantly, adding to its three hotels (the original Sun City Hotel, the upmarket Cascades and the family-style Cabanas) with the construction of the magnificent Lost City with its luxury Palace of the Lost City hotel.

There are numerous attractions within the double complex. Sun City houses dazzling gambling halls, the extravaganza

ABOVE, AND PREVIOUS PAGES The opulent Palace of the Lost City. OPPOSITE A Soweto shebeen (tavern). BELOW Part of the famed Sterkfontein Caves complex. BOTTOM Inside Nelson Mandela's old home in Soweto.

ABOVE Improbable as it sounds, one can body-surf in the great interior – at the Lost City's Valley of the Waves.
BELOW Crocodiles are an unusual hazard at the Lost City golf course's 13th hole.
BOTTOM The Lost City course, designed by veteran golfer Gary Player, is among the country's finest.

theatre, shops, restaurants, nighspots, bars, cinemas and much else, and it overlooks the 18-hole Gary Player Golf Course. The massive building next door is the Superbowl, venue for ambitious concerts, beauty pageants, world championship boxing events, banquets and spectacles of many different kinds.

The Palace of the Lost City

The Palace is generally recognised as one of the world's most opulent and imaginatively conceived hotels, the designers, builders and decorators sparing no expense in its creation. Furniture and fittings are custom-made and state-of-the-art; the entrance is an immense gateway with a much-larger-than-life sculptural backdrop of a cheetah in full cry after a herd of leaping impala. A circular fountain of bronze sable-heads greets you in the courtyard. Marble-and-crystal-tiled floors lead out on to the Crystal Court, which has floor-to-ceiling windows, a massive chandelier shaped like palm fronds, and a centrepiece of bronze elephants.

Waterworld

A vast man-made lake situated in front of the Cascades Hotel offers just about any water sport you could possibly want or even imagine, including parasailing, waterskiing (and waterskiing lessons), jet-skis, pedal boats, self-drive boats, family motorboats and bumper boats. There are instructors on hand for most of the activities.

The Valley of Waves

For many visitors, this provides the highlight of their stay. Here, unlikely as it may sound, realistic turquoise breakers make their way across the enormous, concrete-floored, lake-like pool to crash onto a white, palm-fringed beach, and it's all great fun. Towels can be hired, backrests dot the beach and surrounds, and waiters are on hand with their drinks trays. Behind the 'beach' is a set of five water-slides, the one known as the 'Temple of Courage' a death-defying 70-metre plunge down a steep mountainside and into the sparkling pool below. There's also the 'Sacred River Ride', a gentle bob along a channel that winds around the island, and the 'Mamba Ride', which takes you 'underground' for a short distance.

Sun City for Children

For all its sophistication, the complex is well geared for families.

Qualified staff organise activities throughout the day at Kamp Kwena Fort, a well-run holiday programme for youngsters. There is also mini-golf, a fully equipped children's playground, an aviary, a small mine where the little ones can dig for treasure, and an animal farm. Twice a day, the South African Birds of Prey Centre gives a flight demonstration of the magnificent buzzards, eagles and other large raptors of the region.

Botanical Gardens Tours

Five trails wind through the superlative grounds each day. A decade ago, an impressive 260 000 plantings, including more than 6 000 trees, were introduced. Today the gardens are haven for about 3 200 different species, and you can easily imagine that you're in a tropical jungle and not, as reality tells you, in the middle of a volcanic crater. A variety of habitats have been established, ranging from rainforests through wetlands to coastal vegetation. The entire area has been awarded Botanical Garden status.

The Beach Tour takes rather more than an hour to complete and explores the Crocodile Valley, the Royal Staircase to the Valley of Waves and the Monkey Spring Plaza. The focus is on the coastal and tropical plants. Look out for green pigeons in the big wild fig trees. The

Spider Web Trail, geared to the young and adventurous, starts at the Cycad Forest, crossing the Swing Bridge before making its way through the Rain Forest and down to Hippo Gorge. From there it leads to the Jacaranda Forest, the Royal Staircase and the Valley of Waves.

The Cascades Gardens and Waterworld Tour leads you past the many stunning water features (stocked with indigenous fish) and through the aviaries and forest to the 18th green of the Gary Player Golf Course and Country Club. It ends at the clubhouse. The Baobab Tour is a little more strenuous, taking up to two hours and focusing on the large and weird baobab trees, largest of which weighs about 40 tons. Highlights of the Lost City Croc Pit Tour are various euphorbias, aloes and other desert-type plants and the crocodile 'hazard' at the golf course's 13th hole.

Pilanesberg National Park

Pilanesberg is probably one of only two 'big five' reserves in the country that is in a malaria-free area (the other is Shamwari, in the Eastern Cape). The 580-square-kilometre park, which is set in an eroded volcano thought to be more than 100 million years old, is virtually next door to Sun City.

During Operation Genesis, one of the largest game relocation operations ever carried out, more than 6 000 animals, including all the 'big five' (lion, leopard, elephant, rhino, buffalo) were moved into Pilanesberg from various parts of the subcontinent. An impressive array of antelope and plains animals – among them zebra and giraffe – browse or graze on the open grasslands and in the thickly wooded gorges. There is an abundant bird life. Wildlife-viewers have a fine selection of water holes and hides from which to choose.

Park accommodation is available in lodges, chalets and camp sites, many situated close to the four entrances. Near the big Manyane Camp is an area specially fenced in for self-guided walks. There are also conducted trails, led by an armed ranger, and day and night drives.

A number of up-market, privately owned and rather luxurious game lodges – Bakubang, Tshukudu and Kwa Maritane among them – are situated on the

periphery of the park, as are smaller guest lodges, some of whose operators take clients into the Pilanesberg to observe the park's celebrated wild dog programme in action. The highlight is feeding time, when an antelope carcass is deposited in the big boma area for the animals.

An especially inviting though perhaps rather expensive 'tour' is by hot-air balloon. Flights usually leave early in the morning – you're collected from wherever you are staying and driven to the launch site in the middle of the park – and the journey lasts about four hours, during which you drift serenely over the veld, watching the wild game going about its business and enjoying the magnificent African scenery. Breakfast is served at one of the private game lodges, where you receive a 'first flight certificate' before being returned to your home base.

TOP Among the Pilanesberg park's big attractions are the relatively relaxed elephants and wild dogs.
ABOVE Game Trackers Wildlife Adventures has expert guides to take you around, although many visitors choose to self-drive.

USEFUL CONTACTS

Soweto Township Tours
Jimmy' s Face to Face
Tel: 011 331 6109
Fax: 011 331 5388
face2face@pixie.co.za
www.face2face.co.za

Cradle of Humankind World Heritage Site
Tel: 011 957 0034
Fax: 011 957 0344
infotour@fast.co.za
www.valleyofancestors.co.za

Sun City Central Reservations
Tel: 014 557 8100/011 780 7800
Fax: 011 780 7443
www.suninternational.com

Pilanesburg National Park
Tel: 014 555 5351
Fax: 014 555 5525
nwptb@iafrica.com
www.tourismnorthwest.co.za

Tshukudu Lodge
Tel: 011 302 3802
Fax: 011 302 3868
hotels@legacyhotels.co.za
www.legacyhotels.co.za

Game Trackers
Tel: 014 552-1561
Fax: 014 552 1343

Hot-air Ballooning
Pilanesberg Balloon Safaris
Tel: 014 552 1552

One of Tshukudu Lodge's deluxe bathrooms.

The Golden Hills

Southeastern Free State

*T*he southeastern segment of the Free State, which shares a border with the mountain kingdom of Lesotho, is one of South Africa's best-kept tourism secrets. A patchwork of rich farms and orchards heavy with fruit grace a quite breathtaking landscape backed by the towering Maloti Mountains. Between the Golden Gate in the east and Ladybrand in the west the countryside rises in a series of picturesquely eroded sandstone hills and grand cliffs dotted with caves that the early San people and, later, herders of sheep and cattle took shelter.

Southeastern Free State

Golden Gate Highlands National Park, Clarens, Fouriesburg
and Ficksburg, Marquard/Clocolan, Ladybrand

The nature of this lovely region is determined largely by its sandstone overlay, the rock of the weathered hills combining with iron oxides to create a multi-coloured wonderland of reds and oranges, yellows and golds. From this rock, too, buildings ranging from the humblest of homes to the grandest of mansions have been fashioned to bring solid comfort to their occupants – and pleasure to the eye of the visitor.

TOP Brandwag Camp at Golden Gate Highlands National Park overlooks The Sentinel, a huge sandstone outcrop that glows pink and orange in the afternoon light. ABOVE The trail to Echo Caves is short and easy when compared to some of Golden Gate's more strenuous walks. PREVIOUS PAGES The view from the road between Clarens and Fouriesburg.

GOLDEN GATE HIGHLANDS NATIONAL PARK

The park ranks among the country's top attractions – and it's easily accessible. Nestled in the foothills of the towering Maloti Mountains 320 kilometres from Johannesburg, 390 kilometres from Durban and 305 kilometres from Bloemfontein, it occupies a conveniently central position on the major tourist routes. The name is taken from one of its most prominent features, a massive and weirdly sculpted cliff face, and more generally from the various shades of gold that colour the great sandstone outcrops that dominate the countryside.

The Golden Gate itself, the 'gateway' to the park, actually comprises two gigantic sandstone rocks that stand 76 metres high and burn with lustrous luminescence in the late evening or early morning sunshine. Elsewhere there are

other great buttresses, and mushroom-shaped outcrops, pretty streams, deep cave shelters, and grassy hillsides covered in wild flowers that wave their heads gently in the breezes of spring and summer. In winter, snow often covers the landscape, topping the hills with glistening white flakes and turning the waterfalls to ice.

This beautiful, 12 000-hectare expanse of highland habitat is home to a number of wild animals ranging from the tiny oribi to the giant eland and, in between, grey rhebuck, blesbok, springbok, black wildebeest and Burchell's or plains zebra. Many small nocturnal creatures, such as aardwolfs, porcupines and African wild cats, also make their home here, but they tend to be elusive. More commonly seen are the marsh and Cape grey mongooses, spotted genets, striped polecats, black-backed jackals and, surprisingly, Cape clawless otters. On your drive through the park you'll also spot large chacma baboons grubbing around for insects and digging for roots on the hillside.

And then there are the birds. The park is in 'big sky country', the perfect place for observing a variety of raptors ranging from black eagles to jackal buzzards. On the rocky ledges of the steep sandstone cliffs nest the rare bald ibis and bearded vulture. Closer to the ground, keep an eye out for blue cranes, South Africa's national bird, which is also rare, and for common guinea fowls. When picking over the grass-covered hillsides you may well spot long-legged, predatory secretary birds.

The camp sites and outcrops are patronised by rock pigeons. Wild flowers put on a colourful springtime show when watsonias, arum lilies, red-hot pokers and an array of bulbs and herbs burst into bloom in August and September.

There are two rest camps in the park. Glen Reenen, the more rustic of the venues, has bungalows, attractive camp and caravan sites and a scenic picnic spot for day visitors. Brandwag offers hotel accommodation as well as fully-equipped cottages, a restaurant, cocktail bar, coffee shop and laundromat. A small shop at Brandwag sells basic necessities.

For those who like to ramble, walk or hike, there are a number of inviting routes from which to choose, including the Rhebok Trail, which takes two days to complete and has overnight accommodation in a hut kitted out with cooking facilities, firewood and drinking water. The trail is moderately difficult: it runs over the mountain, crossing streams and kloofs, and there are spectacular views along the way. You can also hire mounts and explore the park, with or without a guide, on horseback. Guided horse-trails leave from Brandwag.

Basotho Cultural Village

You'll find this 'living museum' – established to give visitors an insight into the fascinations of Sotho culture and lifestyle – on the road approaching Golden Gate from the east.

A guide will accompany you through the village, starting at a rather primitive hut. From here you follow a trail that winds through the cluster of homesteads,

each depicting a different aspect of or era on the Sotho cultural landscape. One of them illustrates, for example, the point at which the Sotho first decorated the exteriors of their houses; another when they later began to build more sophisticated dwellings.

Visitors are also entertained and enlightened by performances of indigenous music and demonstrations of clay pot-making, hut-building and decorating, cooking, and, most delightfully, of traditional games. There is also, usually, an invitation to sample Sotho food and home-brewed sorghum beer.

A traditional healer is often in attendance, and apart from watching him 'throw the bones', he will also (on request) take you on a two-hour trail, explaining the nature and uses of indigenous medicinal plants en route.

An audio-visual show is laid on at the visitors' centre. There's also a curio shop, a small restaurant and a tea garden that serves snacks.

Rustic, but comfortable, accommodation is available just outside the village. The huts are built of sandstone and offer stunning views over the hills of Golden Gate Highlands National Park. Visitors either cater for themselves or eat at the village restaurant.

Bokpoort Guest Farm

Located on the road between Golden Gate and Clarens, this pleasant place has been in the Roos family for four generations. It's an unpretentious,

ABOVE Grey rhebok occur in the Golden Gate Highlands National Park, but they are not all that common and tend to be shy and elusive.
BELOW A pony, a blanket and a conical straw hat are inseparable from the traditional Basotho man. The Basotho Cultural Village, to the east of Golden Gate, offers an insight into this people's heritage.

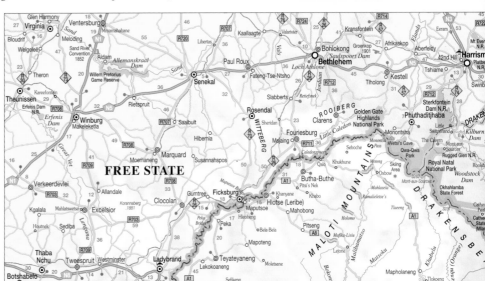

TOP *Cosmos covers the Free State's hills and roadsides in early autumn.*
ABOVE *Fossil-hunting in the Clarens area.*
BELOW *Patterns and colours of Basotho blankets symbolise aspects of their culture.*

friendly guest farm, which puts its visitors up in converted chicken houses, and the dining room is in the old barn, but it's comfortable, standards are high and the service excellent.

Highlight of your stay is a ride along the Snowy River Horse Trail, rated as one of the loveliest in the country: the scenery en route is quite awesome and the people you're with are splendid companions. There's sometimes a lively barn dance, evoking something of the old pioneer days, on the evening of your arrival; riders start at the farm and head off through the surrounding farmlands into the wilderness areas of the Maloti foothills, overnighting under the stars in warmer weather, or in old (converted) herder's shacks or barns in the winter. Dinner is cooked over an open fire. The actual duration of the trail is left to the riders: it can be anything from a couple of hours to two, three or even five days' long, depending on their preferences and time available.

The owner of the farm is a qualified riding instructor, and he and his wife breed mustangs, known as Basotho ponies in South Africa. The ponies are generally tough and sturdy, and they're familiar with every path in the valley, so they provide the ideal mount for both experienced and inexperienced riders. Bokpoort also offers day rides.

BLANKETS FROM THE BASOTHO

The fascinating little De Jager and diMezza Blanket Shop began life, in 1946, as a general trading store serving the local Sotho community. It is still run by the daughters of the original owner, but today it specialises in distinctive, traditional Basotho blankets, and is a popular stopover for foreign and local tourists interested in both the culture of the Sotho people and the wonderful wares they fashion.

Although the Basotho blanket is an everyday item of clothing for many Basotho these days, it once indicated a very lowly status. It's now worn for a variety of different and distinctive reasons, most notably on ceremonial and ritualistic occasions. The beautiful colours and designs captivate the eye, and fascinate the mind with their symbolic meaning. Among the most popular patterns are the *poone,* or maize design, a corncob motif, which signifies fertility, and the cabbage leaf, a symbol of prosperity. Specific patterns are worn only by royalty and by headmen.

The two elderly sisters who own and run the shop also sell a variety of more modern style blankets, made from synthetic fibres, together with 'special editions' – for instance, those made for the Lesotho Royal Wedding in February 2000.

CLARENS

The town, set among the grand hills of the southeastern Free State, has become a haven for artists and crafters from all around the country. Most of the buildings are attractive, built of sandstone cut from the mountains. For visitors, there are some good small restaurants and coffee shops, and plenty of quaint, if somewhat cutesy, galleries and craft shops selling pottery, paintings, woodcarvings, weavings and curios. An art festival is held annually.

Other attractions of the wider area include some wonderful trails, and ancient San rock-art sites.

Dinosaur Trails and Fossil-hunting Expeditions

Geologists believe that at one point about 260 million years ago, when Africa was still part of the supercontinent known as Gondwana, the area around what is now Clarens comprised a large lake system that alternately flooded and dried up. And over the millennia a variety of animals and plants became trapped in the layers of clay, calcrete and other soils, leaving their remains to be discovered by their far-distant human heirs.

Dr Gideon Groenewald is Clarens's 'Dinosaur Man', and to take part in one of his exploratory excursions through the hills and mountains is excitement indeed. On these, it's almost certain that you will come across fossils of invertebrates such as worms, crabs, snails and other mud-dwelling organisms dating back about 230 to 220 million years. You'll probably also find such vertebrates as fish, amphibians, even some of the early reptiles and, less likely but quite possible, dinosaur droppings (coprolites), dinosaur teeth and perhaps dinosaur eggs with embryos still embedded.

Tours begin with a fascinating explanation of the geology and geological history of the region. This introduction is followed by a drive out to a likely fossil site in the mountains. Visitors on previous trips have found a number of dog-like *Tritylodon* skulls.

Gideon also runs five-day 4x4 dinosaur trails and fossil-hunting expeditions in the area farther east, into the beautiful northern regions of KwaZulu-Natal.

FOURIESBURG AND FICKSBURG

Saltpeterkrans or Fertility Cave

There's a sign on the road that winds between Clarens and Fouriesburg indicating the Anglo-Boer War site of Surrender Hill. This is also the turnoff to the largest rock overhang in the southern hemisphere. Apparently the shelter was originally used by early San people and later by the local Sotho herders, but in recent decades it has been taken over by traditional healers, wise men who come here from all over the country to study and perform ancient spiritual rites. It is also believed by many African people that women who find it difficult to conceive would, after a visit to this hallowed place, be cured of their barrenness through the mediation of a healer.

It is about a 20-minute hike, from the roadside spot where you leave your car, to the overhang. The route, which takes you through private property (make sure that you close farm gates behind you), follows a beautiful little stream into a kloof flanked by high sandstone cliffs. The narrow crossing can be rather difficult to negotiate during the rainy season, so be prepared to wade through the water. Once over the crossing, it is a fairly steep but very short walk up to the shelter which, enormous though it is, is hidden by a massive pile of rocks and can easily be missed. Better still, hire someone to show you the way. Names and contact details of guides are listed at the local tourism office.

A number of healers, clothed in traditional attire, reside *in situ* while in training. Each living area is demarcated by a low stone wall.

Rock concerts have been held, on an ad hoc basis, at the shelter in recent times. Locals in Clarens or Fouriesburg will be able to give you details.

Rustler's Valley Music Festival

A popular open-air music festival takes place each Easter deep in Rustler's Valley, about 18 kilometres off the R26 between Fouriesburg and Ficksburg. Here hundreds of people spend four days camping out, listening to the sounds and enjoying the splendid natural environment. Visitors can also attend one of the regular drum circles or a workshop and demonstration on the making and playing of traditional African marimbas. Fire-dancers, clowns and jugglers keep the crowds enthralled at the open-air market.

For those who don't want to camp, there are self-catering chalets on the farm.

Meiringskloof Nature Reserve

The reserve is set on the outskirts of Fouriesburg, in a wonderfully green and shady valley tucked between golden-orange sandstone cliffs. Self-catering cottages and grassy caravan and camp sites are pleasantly scattered among the trees. The main attraction is the hike to Holkrans, a massive overhang in which Fouriesburg's entire population of women and children took refuge during the Anglo-Boer War of 1899–1902.

ABOVE Rolling wheat fields are as familiar an eastern Free State scene as are the sandstone cliffs.
BELOW Most of the walks and trails at Meiringskloof wind in and around rock formations like these, worn away by the action of water over millennia.
BOTTOM Saltpeterkrans is a huge overhang, with profound religious significance for many of South Africa's peoples.

41

ABOVE Sterkfontein Dam is one of the largest in the country and a fine venue for windsurfers, particularly in late winter when strong winds blow.
BELOW October and November is cherry time in the eastern Free State, when the fruit ripens and cherry wines and liqueurs are made.
BOTTOM A unique place of worship is the Cave Chapel at the Modderpoort Priory.

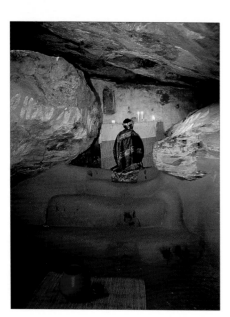

Beyond the 'cave', the path leads into an enchanting crevice through which a stream flows. Millennia of water erosion have moulded the crevice into an enormous tunnel which, though open to the sky, is difficult to detect from the grasslands above. One exits the tunnel either by climbing the chain ladder (you'll find this at the end of the track) or by walking back and across the wooden bridge to the resort.

Ficksburg Cherry Festival

The region is famed for its fine agricultural produce generally and, in particular, for its cherries. Cool winter temperatures and just the right kind of soils combine to nurture splendid crops of this fruit – a relatively unusual one in southern Africa.

The cherry season lasts for about a month from the third week in October, and it's preceded (in September) by a quite breathtaking show of snowy-white cherry blossoms. The annual Ficksburg Cherry Festival, held in mid- or late November, has been running for almost 60 years. Most of the orchards are tucked away on the deep, well-drained soils of the mountain slopes, so to see the blossoms you'll have to make a small detour onto dirt roads.

CLOCOLAN AND MARQUARD
Ben Nevis Cherry Cellar and Tea Garden

About three kilometres off the R707 between Clocolan and Marquard is an attractive cherry and asparagus farm that produces, among much else, a fine selection of cherry wines and liqueurs.

Each season brings a different farm activity, but one can tour the place at any time of the year, enjoy a wine-tasting session and then excellent farm refreshments of one sort or another. There's a small tea garden under the shady trees; a traditional Free State barbecue can be arranged or, if you prefer, picnic baskets prepared for you in advance of your visit.

September to November is the asparagus season, November is cherry-picking time, plums and peaches ripen in December; vegetables and peaches again are harvested in January and February, April is the month for olives. In winter, the pumpkin seeds are washed and dried.

Visitors can also embark on a wonderful 'adventure' walk through groves of indigenous trees, past eye-catching sandstone formations and overhangs graced by San rock art.

If you've packed a sleeping bag, you're welcome to stay over in an old farmhouse on the property. Here you will be overwhelmed by the best of Free State country hospitality. The tariff covers bed and breakfast; supper on request.

Evening Star

This is the rather charming name of a farm originally (1870) established by settlers in the region and later taken over by the Catholic Order of Mary, who built a monastery. St Leo's College, the first school in the Free State to offer secondary education, was then founded just east of the farm.

Later still, Evening Star was bought, and is still owned, by the Cloete family, who have restored the old monastery. Most of the buildings are of beautifully hewn sandstone and many still have floors made, in the original way, from cattle dung.

The farm, a declared national monument, is part of the surrounding Metsiawang Conservancy. A ceramic studio and gallery is housed in one of the old outbuildings. There's also a tea garden that serves, among other things, the most refreshing of home-made lemonades. Accommodation comprises a self-catering chalet perched halfway up the mountain behind the monastery, overlooking the wild slopes of the rolling farmlands. A food basket can be provided on request. It's all very romantic, and an ideal honeymoon venue.

There is also an enticing three-hour hiking trail that offers breathtaking views. Indigenous plants are identified along the route.

Modderpoort Priory

In 1869, Anglican missionaries set up home in a small cave, product of a massive sandstone rock-fall, outside the town Ladybrand, but these natural surrounds never really suited the priests' purposes and were eventually replaced by the lovely sandstone buildings that later became St Augustine's Mission and the Modderpoort Priory. The cave is still there, though: it has long served as a kind of annex chapel. It is said that, during the apartheid years, the chapel was used as a hideaway by ANC activists on their escape route into Lesotho.

The Priory's cemetery hosts an unusual grave – it belongs to a famous Basotho prophetess, Anna Mantshupa Makheta, who died in 1904. A contemporary and relative of the great Basotho leader Moshoeshoe, her predictions (many of which were fulfilled) gave her great status as a leader and healer. Africans in their thousands make the pilgrimage to Modderpoort to pay homage and ask Makheta's blessing. They visit the cave chapel, her grave and a water well where she is said to have received many of her prophetic visions. Makheta's grave is unmistakable: it's the only one with a Victorian Gothic tombstone covered in gifts of flowers, red clay bowls, coins, beads and tiny pyramids of maize.

LADYBRAND

This pretty little town, set in the western part of the southeastern Free State region, is surrounded by rocky sandstone ridges and boasts a number of well-preserved, restored sandstone buildings.

About 22 kilometres from Ladybrand is the farm Tandjiesberg, famed for its San rock art, and most notably for one of the few authentic (although now terribly faded) San depictions of what many believe is a white woman. During a recent fire, some of the painted walls of the cave were destroyed. However, it has since been patched up and one can still see a few of the magnificent artworks.

Rose Cottage Cave, which is under the administration of the University of the Witwatersrand's Department of Archaeology, is another of the area's important caves, used for human habitation over the long millennia between a 100 000 and 10 000 years ago. There is evidence that at one time or another its occupants hunted animals commonly found today, such as eland, zebra and black wildebeest, and also species that are now extinct – the quagga, for example, and the bluebuck and Cape horse. Some of the cave's artwork depict freshwater fish of a kind that has never occurred in the Ladybrand area. Even more intriguing, perhaps, is the ancient cowrie shell unearthed – it's from the eastern seaboard, prompting archaeologists to speculate that our early Stone Age ancestors were either travellers or had excellent trade networks.

TOP The ancient rock art at Tandjiesberg near Ladybrand is especially well preserved. ABOVE Many folk still visit the grave of the prophetess Anna Mantshupa Makheta to pray, pay homage and ask her blessing.

USEFUL CONTACTS

Highlands Tourist and Information Centre
Tel: 058 256 1542
Fax: 058 256 1643
clarens@bhm.dorea.co.za

South African National Parks
Tel: 012 343 1991
Fax: 012 343 0905
reservations@parks-sa.co.za
www.parks-sa.co.za

Golden Gate Highlands National Park
Brandwag Camp
Tel: 058-255 0012
Fax: 058 255 0928

Glenreenen Camp
Tel: 058 255 0075
058 255 0919
www.parks-sa.co.za

Basotho Cultural Village
Tel: 058 721 0300
Fax: 058 721 0304
basotho@dorea.co.za
www.dorea.co.za/ecotourism

Gideon Groenewald Dinosaur and Fossil Expeditions
Tel: 058 256 1314
Cell: 082 829 4978
gideon@dorea.co.za

De Jager and diMezza Blanket Shop
Tel: 058 256 1313

Modderpoort Priory
Tel/Fax: 051 924 3318
chaslange@freemail.absa.co.za

Ben Nevis Cherry Cellar and Tea Garden
Tel/Fax: 051 943 0031

Meiringskloof Nature Park
Tel: 058 223 0067
Cell: 082 896 4956

Bokpoort Guest Farm and Horse Trails
Tel: 058 256 1181
Cell: 083 628 5055
horses@bokpoort.co.za
www.bokpoort.co.za

Ladybrand and Maloti Tourist Office
Tel: 051 924 5131
Fax: 051 924 2556
Cell: 082 690 2489
malotiinfo@xsinet.co.za

Rustler's Valley
Tel: 051 933 3939
Fax: 051 933 3286
Cell: 082 854 8796
wemad@rustlers.co.za
www.rustlers.co.za

Evening Star
Cell: 083 305 0658
Fax: 051 943 7147

Some of the comfortable chalets at Brandwag Camp.

Sun and Sea

Durban City and Surrounds

*D*urban has just about everything for the leisure-bent visitor: a balmy, subtropical climate, splendid beaches, a warm sea, surfing waves that are internationally renowned, good hotels, restaurants, glittering shopping malls, lively theatres, museums, sporting venues, lushly green parks and gardens, and much else. In fact, Durban is South Africa's premier domestic holiday destination. It's also the country's biggest and busiest port city, and the place where the cultures – Zulu and Indian, Hindu, Christian and Muslim, white and brown – meet and mix in a marvellous human kaleidoscope.

Durban City and Surrounds

The City, Cultural Durban, Umgeni River Bird Park, Umhlanga Rocks

Durban is the principal urban centre of the country's eastern region, a bustling, hustling hub of industrial, commercial and leisure activity that grew from the function for which it was founded – as the maritime gateway to the subcontinent. Prime focus for the holidaymaker is the six-kilometre seafront stretch known as the Golden Mile.

TOP A few of Durban's fishermen still use beachfront rowing boats to drag their nets out to sea.
ABOVE Durban, with its myriad hotels, restaurants and pubs, comes alive at night.
*PREVIOUS PAGES The **sun-blessed** city in the early evening.*

Durban is a truly African city, and one of great contrasts – a vibrant mix of sophisticated shopping centres, galleries, theatres, up-market hotels, dining and wining venues and nighspots on the one hand; raucous street vendors, shacklands and poverty on the other.

Just north of the city is Umhlanga Rocks, a stylish resort town. To the south, towards and beyond Amanzimtoti, there are superb stretches of sand and good, safe bathing. Lifeguards are on duty on all the area's popular beaches, particularly during peak season and over weekends.

THE CITY
The Golden Mile
Durban's promenade stretches six dazzling kilometres along the coast, from Rutherford Street in the south to Playfair Road on North Beach, and there is easy and safe access to sand and sea. The promenade, lined by an almost endless rank of hotels, shops, eateries and entertainment centres, is busy, particularly over weekends and during holidays as people of all ages come to bathe in the pools, jog, skateboard, cycle, rollerblade, shoot basketball hoops, play beach volleyball or just stroll along and enjoy the action. Pedestrian piers jut out into the ocean; the beaches are broad, golden and inviting; the surf often challenging.

July is the time of the Ocean Action Festival, when the Golden Mile takes on a wonderful carnival atmosphere. Events include the longest-running surfing competition in the world, once known as The Gunston 500 and now as the Mr Price Pro, and a prominent feature of the international surfing calendar. Associated with the event is an arduous iron-man contest, and body-boarding and jet-ski competitions. Secondary, but no less entertaining, are the beach volleyball and beach soccer matches and kickboxing demonstrations. During the festival, the promenade is packed with surfers from around the world. Girls in bikinis decorate the area, and stalls sell everything from beach gear to bunny-chow (a traditional Durban food consisting of a hollowed out half-loaf of bread filled with curry).

Learning to surf is time-consuming, and takes some effort, but it's a lot of fun and, once you're proficient, the skill can enhance your beach holiday enormously. Sea-kayaking tuition is available, whatever the weather and sea conditions, at the Chalupsky Paddling and Adventure School in the protected area at Vetchies Beach, on the far southern end of the Golden Mile near the Point Waterfront.

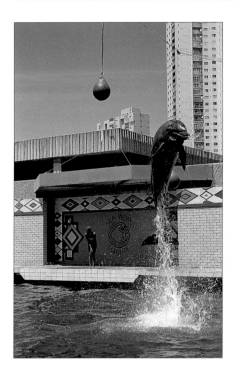

Waterfront and Harbour

Durban's harbour mouth is a fine place to pass the time of day watching ships great and small, and the fishermen and, especially at night, the dolphins that are sometimes visible in the harbour lights. Drinks and a meal can be enjoyed at one of the quayside restaurants. There's also a weekend fleamarket and tea garden in the open promenade area.

The waterfront tourist development is still at the fledgling stage; planned are an enormous new theme aquarium, jazz clubs, more coffee shops and various entertainment venues.

The B.A.T Centre

Still in the harbour area but towards the city and near the yacht basin is Durban's renowned B.A.T. (Bartle Arts Trust) Centre, established in 1995 to encourage KwaZulu-Natal's (and particularly the city's) rich cultural heritage. The centre supports visual and performing artists who may otherwise not have the chance to produce, practise or exhibit their work.

Neatly enough, the building resembles a bat in flight when seen from across the bay.

The front part of the B.A.T. Centre houses a coffee bar, restaurant and some African art and craft outlets; the back part accommodates a theatre, artists', musicians' and dancers' studios, and art

and craft galleries. Night classes and demonstrations are held regularly. On weekend nights (starting with Friday-evening jazz) the place becomes an exuberant hive of activity, hosting shows, live music, local theatre productions and African film and video festivals.

Sea World

Durban's Sea World, the Dolphinarium, and the attached Oceanographic Research Institute (ORI) have been deeply involved in marine conservation for decades, adding hugely to the fund of knowledge about South Africa's coastal waters and their inhabitants – and, at the same time, introducing the public to the wonders of the ocean.

Sea World is a great place to spend a windy or rainy day – or any day for that matter. Both Sea World and the ORI will be moving to their new premises on Durban's waterfront.

One of the complex's main attractions is the shark tank, but there are other exhibits aplenty – beautiful corals, poisonous firefish and stonefish, reef tanks teeming with enormous bonito, kingfish, grunter and much else.

Scuba divers regularly feed the massive (but gentle) stingrays and the sea turtles by hand.

Dolphin, seal and penguin shows are held each day in the building next door, and children are sometimes allowed to pet and feed the dolphins.

*LEFT The **much-loved** Sea World dolphin show.*
ABOVE The Warwick Triangle's muthi (medicine) market, Africa's largest.
BELOW Murals brighten the B.A.T. Centre.

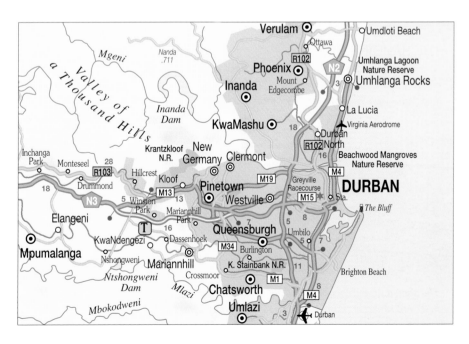

ABOVE *Among the most colourful of Durban's beachfront features are the man-pulled rickshas, a tourist attraction that started as a functional transport service in the 1890s.*

CULTURAL DURBAN
Victoria Street

The Victoria Street-Warwick Triangle area is one of the most vibrant parts of the city, the location of (among other things) the Indian Market, which is housed in a large purple building – where you'll find shops and stalls inviting you to bargain for anything from Malawian carvings through Hindu flame-lamps, beaded alice-bands, fabrics, pots and pans to Indian brassware. Of special note are the spice merchants with their piles of bright red and orange curry and masala mixes bearing evocative names ('mother-in-law's tongue' is one). Their aromas, mingled with incense, permeate the entire building.

Next door is the fascinating fish and meat market, where everything from sheep's heads to odd-looking deep-sea fish is on show and for sale. Make an early start to be in time for the arrival of the fresh fish, crabs, squid, crayfish (rock lobster) and prawns brought in from Mozambique, the Cape and other coastal regions.

Across the way is the Warwick Triangle Fresh Produce Market, which, again, is best visited early in the mornings when the fruit, vegetables and flowers are brought from around the country in large trucks.

It's a frenetic scene – noisy, colourful, very unlike that of the rather clinical, sterile chain stores located in the big modern malls – as trolley pushers, traders and shoppers jostle for the freshest items. Some of the vendors belong to families of market gardeners who have been in the business for generations.

Right alongside is Africa's largest Muthi Market (*muthi* means 'medicine'), where a large variety of plants and animal parts are sold by informal traders and traditional healers. Mixtures of bark, plants, herbs and bulbs are chopped into colourful concoctions or sold in individual pieces. Prominent among the stalls are those that offer sometimes gruesome-looking animal parts, which is not what the average tourist expects to find in a modern city. Crocodile teeth, skulls and skins, for example, are displayed alongside birds' wings and beaks, snake skins, shells, bones and the occasional monkey's paw.

Everyone here is friendly and helpful; and it's quite safe to venture to and around the market on your own (or hire a guide through the Durban tourism offices). One can also ask a sangoma – a spiritual healer – to 'throw the bones' for you, although many of the practitioners are from the remote rural areas and do not speak English very well.

Jumma Musjid Mosque

The sound of the Muslim call to prayer – through the loudspeakers of the southern hemisphere's largest mosque – can be heard at regular times throughout the day. The mosque, a beautiful golden-domed structure, is situated on the corner of Grey and Queen streets. It was built in the late 1880s by folk whose families had been brought in from the Indian subcontinent to work the great sugar plantations of the coastal region.

Visitors are welcome to tour sections of the graceful building. Women should wear a long skirt, and a top that keeps the shoulders covered. For those not appropriately dressed, robes are provided at the entrance. You are asked to observe custom and leave your shoes outside.

A tour takes in the architecture, the baths and the large hall where men pray, together with a brief explanation of some of the basic Muslim beliefs. Women of the faith usually worship at home, although there is a separate section of the mosque set aside for them (this is not part of the tour).

THE SARDINE RUN

During July, KwaZulu-Natal's southern coast is the venue for one of nature's most exciting and mysterious phenomena – the annual sardine run, when millions of these little fish migrate northwards in massive shoals before heading out to sea and

The annual sardine run brings out the best, and worst, in those involved.

disappearing off into the blue, destination unknown. Quite often the shoals beach themselves, perhaps in an effort to escape predators, perhaps because they are driven ashore by current and tide. These occasions trigger a hilarious frenzy of activity as onlookers lose all sense of dignity and rush *en masse* into the water with buckets, nets, plastic bags, basins, raised skirts or anything else they can use to scoop and hold the fish.

The sardine run has become a major tourist attraction, bringing visitors to the coast from all over the world.

Hindu Temples

Durban's Hindu community, many of whose members are also descended from 19th-century indentured labourers, worship in a number of graceful temples. The Shree Ambalvanar Alayam Second River Temple in Bellair Road, Cato Manor, is one of the oldest and most famous (it is in fact a declared national monument). Brightly painted depictions of the Hindu gods Vishnu, Shiva, Ganesha and others adorn the exterior of the elaborate building, whose entrance is tiled in traditional patterns. The beautiful old doors were salvaged from another temple that was washed away during the massive floods of 1875.

The temples serve as the focal points of festivals such as Kavadi and Ratha Yatra, during some of which devotees fall into a trance-like state that allows such dramatic physical improbabilities as body-piercing, fire-walking and treading or lying on beds of nails. Everyone, both onlookers and participants in parade and ceremony, dresses in their best traditional Indian attire. But not all the festivals are quite so colourful and exciting, and the Hindu temples are also places where the more sedate routines of prayer and meditation are practised daily.

The suburb of Chatsworth hosts the Hare Krishna movement's magnificent Temple of Understanding, which welcomes visitors. Again, a tour will include a brief introduction to beliefs, a look at the architecture and at the opulent paintings that adorn the strikingly domed interior, where there are cool marble floors, large paintings depicting the life and time of Lord Krishna, tranquillity and the gentle scent of incense. The exterior of the building isn't quite so attractive, but stand back and you'll see the famous golden steeples, which are unique in South Africa.

The temple restaurant, which is situated downstairs, serves delicious vegetarian lunches.

Township Tours

Well over two million people live in Durban's dormitory suburbs, or 'townships', many of which were established in the 1950s, at the height of the apartheid regime.

Although it is generally safe enough to visit these areas, you advised not to wander around on your own, for a number of reasons – here there is a lot of poverty, no proper maps, and roads are not always signposted. Durban tourism offices can arrange tours with good operators. A guide who actually lives in one of the townships is recommended. The tour will usually start at the KwaMuhle Museum, where the exhibits offer an insight into the history of the townships – the pass laws, influx control measures, the infamous 'beerhall system' and so forth. This is followed by a drive out to either Clermont or Lamontville, or both, with a stopover at the partially restored Gandhi Settlement.

ABOVE The enchantment of the East: a Hindu bride on her wedding day.
ABOVE LEFT The figures of Lord Krishna and his entourage are mounted in a beautifully decorated shrine in the main hall of The Temple of Understanding.
BELOW Jumma Musjid Mosque dominates the Grey Street area, its tranquil interior a haven from the bustle of the outside world.

ABOVE The raucous calls of exotic blue-and-gold macaws welcome visitors to the Umgeni River Bird Park.
ABOVE RIGHT The South Beach swimming pool has a backdrop of blue sea, tropical plants and holiday apartments.
BELOW The 13th hole at the Zimbali Golfing Estate looks out over lush vegetation and waterways.
OPPOSITE, ABOVE Part of the bird show at the Umgeni River Bird Park.
OPPOSITE, BELOW Dissection demo at the Sharks Board, Umhlanga Rocks.

Many visitors are unaware that the Mahatma, father of modern India, spent 21 years of his life in Durban. It was here that he started his 'passive resistance' movement, and established a self-help farm and an influential newspaper.

Next stop will be the Ohlanga Institute and Reverend John Dube's grave. Dube was the first president of the African National Congress, a clergyman, teacher, writer, political leader and a great humanitarian. He organised his famed institute on Gandhi's principles of self-sufficiency (the latter's settlement is just across the valley), which became well

known for the excellent education offered to young Africans at a time when formal opportunities were more or less non-existent. Dube bequeathed the land, which overlooks the settlement (it also affords fine views over the city), to the nation.

Thirdly, there is KwaDabeka Hostel, largest in the southern hemisphere (it houses up to 15 000 residents). This part of the tour, which enables you to see first-hand how many South Africans live, usually includes a visit to Ebuhleni, citadel of the estimated 400 000-plus Shembe followers, a prominent sect in Durban's spiritual life. The Shembe, who combine traditional African beliefs with Christianity, express their convictions largely through music and dance; ceremonies and services involve singing, and the playing of long, deep-toned horns called *imbombu* accompanied by Zulu drums. Two important Shembe annual events are the 60-kilometre sacred pilgrimage to the Holy Mountain Ebuhleni (January), and the month-long July festival.

The Campbell Collections

One of the country's premier private collections of African artwork and artefacts are housed in a stately old family home overlooking the city from an elevated position on the high ridge known as The Berea. They are divided into the Killie Campbell Africana Library, which contains the world's most comprehensive store of southeast Africa books (it includes oral, photographic and documentary material), and the William Campbell Picture Collection, a splendid accumulation of works by such African artists as Gerard Bengu, Jabulani Ntuli and SMT Mnguni. The collection also embraces 250 of Barbara Tyrell's artworks, documenting African tribal life, Zulu society and Zulu customs.

Among the most fascinating part of the complex is the Mashu Museum of Ethnology, which contains the region's finest collections of African cultural artefacts. These can be viewed only by appointment, on private guided tours. Visitors are introduced to the life of the Campbell family, founders of the museum, as well as to the splendid works on display.

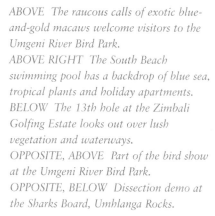

UMGENI RIVER BIRD PARK

One of the first things that strikes you on arrival at the park is the noise – the incessant chattering, chirping and occasional screeching of the birds. The second is that not all the residents are in cages. Much of the area consists of enormous open aviaries where birds fly (almost) free, and where they are easily observable from big overhead wooden walkways in the tree canopy. This is a world-class bird park, with clean, airy and well-kept enclosures and a variety of indigenous and exotic, rare and endangered and colourful species on display. They range in size from large raptors to tiny waxbills.

The free-flight show is held twice a day and is highly entertaining as well as educational. The birds – including the large, ponderous ground hornbills, Cape vultures, gaudy macaws, an African fish eagle, owls, storks and colourful parakeets – put on a wonderful exhibition while their trainers describe some of the many problems of conservation. The show is interactive; children are encouraged to get involved. It is also an opportunity for the public to see rare species such as the wattled and blue cranes. There is an open-air café in the centre of the park.

THE BIRD'S-EYE VIEW OF DURBAN

A wonderful way to see Durban is from the air, and especially on the microlight trips that operate from La Mercy airfield, north of Umhlanga Rocks. The 'flip' lasts about an hour, and will take you down the coast to the Umhlanga Rocks lighthouse before heading up towards Ballito Bay. Weather permitting, in fact, the flight leads right along the coast, over attractive coastal resorts, wide, sandy river estuaries, forests and waving fields of sugar cane.

Helicopter trips are also available.

UMHLANGA ROCKS
The Sharks Board

Durban's Sharks Board, the only organisation of its kind in the world, plays a vital role in both marine conservation and human security – apart

from its research on the sharks of KwaZulu-Natal's offshore waters, it maintains the nets that protect the province's popular swimming beaches.

A visit to the board's premises in Umhlanga Rocks involves a walk around the entrance display cases and the fibreglass models of sharks and dolphins. The walls are covered with newspaper cuttings reporting the many gruesome attacks that occurred along the coast before the nets were set in place. Then there's a powerful, 26-minute audio-visual on the fascinating part sharks play in the marine food chain, a show that dispels many of the horror myths about these primeval creatures. Twice a week the video is followed by the dissection of a shark. Although the ammonia-like smell can be a little overpowering, the internal anatomy is fascinating.

Weather permitting, you can also take an early morning ski-boat trip to observe first-hand how the meshing crews go about servicing the nets off Durban's Golden Mile. Whale- and dolphin-spotting excursions are also on offer in season (May to October).

USEFUL CONTACTS

Tourism KZN
Tel: 031 304 7144
Fax: 031 304 8858
sbu@tourism-kzn.org
www.zulu.org.za

Durban Africa
Tel: 031 304 4934
Fax: 031 304 6196
funinsun@iafrica.com
www.durbanexperiance.co.za

Sea World
Tel: 031 337 3536
Fax: 031 337 2132
seaworld@dbn.lia.net
www.seaworld.org.za

Sea Kayaking
Chalupsky Paddling and
Adventure School
Tel: 031 303 7336
chiarab@chalupsky.com
www.chalupsky.com

Jumma Musjid Mosque
Tel: 031 307 4786

Temple of Understanding
Tel: 031 430 3367

Township Tours
Strelitzia Tours
Tel: 031 266 9480

Black Emerging Tour Operators
Tel: 031 304 7144

The Cambell Collections
Tel: 031 207 3432

Umgeni River Bird Park
Tel: 031 579 4600
Fax: 031 579 4574
urbpmark@ifarica.com
www.umgeniriverbirdpark.co.za

Sharks Board
Tel: 031 566 0400
Boat tours
Cell: 082 403 9206
www.shark.co.za

Microlight and Helicopter Flips
La Mercy Microlights
Tel: 031 561 1685
Cell: 083 597 4222

NAC Helicopters
Tel: 031 564 0176
Fax: 031 563 0037
melanie@nac.co.za

Chopper Flying Services
Tel: 031 563 3347
Fax: 031 563 3226
cfs@icon.co.za
www.helicopter.co.za

Zimbali Golfing Estate's entertainment area.

Barrier of Spears

Midlands and Drakensberg

*T*he main road north from Pietermaritzburg takes you
through the KwaZulu-Natal Midlands, a gentle land
that, in the lush summer months, reminds you of the
classic English countryside. Here there are rolling green
hills, forested valleys, pretty waterfalls, trout-stocked rivers
and streams, small roadside inns and a myriad craft shops,
and pastures that nurture herds of fat dairy cows. Beyond,
though, towering skywards to the west, are the stark
and grandly pinnacled heights of the Drakensberg range,
home to the soaring black eagle and a magnet
for the adventurous climber and hiker.

Midlands and Drakensberg

Howick, Midlands, Drakensberg

The 'Berg, as it is locally known, is a gigantic rampart dividing KwaZulu-Natal's subtropical coastal plain from the great plateau of the southern African interior. To reach it, you travel comfortably through the green and pleasant Midlands, but once there it's difficult to tour the range as a composite 'package' because there is no direct road system linking its southern, central and northern segments, and you have to take a circuitous route to get from one place to another. It is probably better, therefore, to select one region, book in for a night or two and explore the immediate area.

HOWICK

This pleasant town, a short 20-minute drive from Pietermaritzburg, is noted for its enchanting, 95-metre high waterfall, a splendid sight during the summer rainy season but still well worth a visit in the drier months. There is ample parking here, and a safe viewing site from which to watch the water as it plunges over the edge of the rocky cliff. Other visitor amenities include a café and outdoor market, and an information kiosk nearby. One can also reach the base of the falls via the short trail from the Umgeni Valley Nature Reserve, just out of town. The enormous Midmar Dam, upstream from the falls, is hugely popular among weekend watersports enthusiasts, most notably windsurfers, canoeists and water-skiers. There is a small game reserve on the southern shore, and grassy picnic spots and barbecue areas all around the dam. Overnight visitors have a choice of reasonably priced self-catering cottages and camping sites.

MIDLANDS
Midlands Meander

The region between Howick and Mooi River, and east-west from Rietvlei to the Dargle Valley, has been divided into four routes collectively known as the 'Midlands Meander'. The meander is a favourite with locals and tourists alike for the 120 or so arts, crafts and other venues – galleries and gardens, potteries, weaving workshops, flower farms, dairy farms, leather works, coffee shops and country hotels – that welcome you along the various minor roads. There is a quite outstanding variety of high-quality wares on show and on sale.

Some visitors with energy to spare take along their mountain bikes, choose a route from the maps available from garages and other outlets in the wider district, and spend the day pedalling from one spot to another, stopping to enjoy home-made lemon juice or tea and scones in one or another garden along the way. Well-known stop-off points include

Groundcover, famous for its beautifully hand-crafted leather goods (especially shoes), Ian Glenny's Dargle Valley Pottery, and the exquisite hand-dyed and woven throws, rugs and carpets at Shuttleworth Weaving. Also popular are shops selling honey, fresh herbs, smoked trout, home-made cheeses, and pretty, crisp cotton bed-linen and silk duvets. For overnighters there are plenty of cosy bed-and-breakfast establishments, small guesthouses and country inns from which to choose.

DRAKENSBERG OVERVIEW
uKhahlamba-Drakensberg Park

This magnificent conservation area, 300 kilometres long from north to south, a vast 243 000 hectares in extent, protects the great heights and scenically entrancing foothills of the Drakensberg, that spectacular range of mountains that marks the border between South Africa and the lofty kingdom of Lesotho.

The Drakensberg wilderness is a proclaimed World Heritage Site. It is also one of only 23 places in the world that is recognised not just as a site of global natural importance in terms of biodiversity and scenic splendour, but also as an area of unique cultural significance. The Drakensberg is repository for one of the richest displays of rock art in the world, comparable to Machu Picchu in Peru and Uluru-Kata Tjuta (Ayers Rock) in Australia. Here there are more than 600 sites, or 'galleries', of San (Bushman) paintings containing roughly 400 000 individual images. Many have been developed for tourism and can be visited either with a guide or on your own.

The park is informally divided into three sections – north, central and south – linked by some of the best hiking trails in the country. The foothills host a fine selection of resorts, hotels, country inns and guesthouses.

THE SOUTHERN 'BERG

This segment of the Drakensberg – the longest stretch on the map – is in turn divided into two parts, each reached by a different route. The two are linked by gravel roads.

Included in the southern section is Sehlabathebe National Park (which is actually in Lesotho, but will soon be part of the Drakensberg Park), the towering Sani Pass, the Garden Castle foothills area, the small but beautiful Lotheni, Kamberg, Vergelegen (good trout-fishing; few visitor facilities), Himeville and Coleford reserves and, above all, the

ABOVE An eland in the Drakensberg park.
OPPOSITE TOP Munro Bay camp site at Midmar Dam.
OPPOSITE CENTRE Ian Glenny's Dargle Valley pottery.
OPPOSITE BOTTOM The main frieze at the Kamberg reserve's 'gallery' of rock art.
PREVIOUS PAGES Looking towards Champagne Castle and Cathedral Peak.

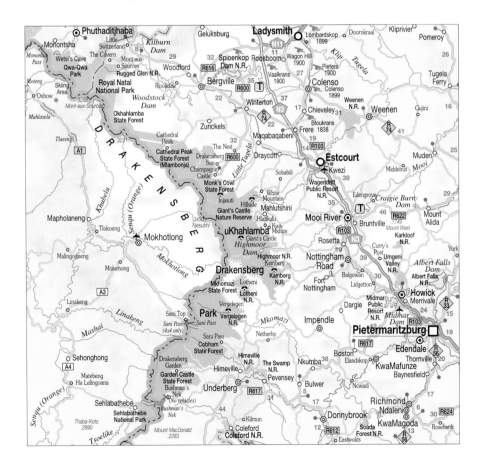

TOP *The steep Sani Pass – best tackled in a four-wheel-drive vehicle.*
ABOVE *The Sani Pass Chalet, situated at the top of the pass, has a cosy pub area from where there are splendid views.*
BELOW *Hikers near Cobham, one of the stopovers on the five-day Giant's Cup Trail.*

splendid Giant's Castle reserve. The principal centres – large and rather charming villages actually – in the southern area are Underberg (on the R617) and, just to the north, Himeville. One reaches the more northern part of the section via the village of Nottingham Road on the R103.

Hikes

The National Hiking Way maintains mountain huts on its routes along the contour paths. There are also cave shelters, camp sites and self-catering cottages run by KZN Wildlife (see page 61), and guided and unguided wilderness foot-trails.

You'll find a number of splendid caves on or just off the wilderness routes, many

bearing evocative names – Sleeping Beauty, Lynx, Grindstone, Yellowwood, and so forth.

Some of the caves serve as overnight shelters for hikers, others are of interest for the rock art they showcase or for their adjacent and attractive waterfalls.

Battle Cave, the site of San paintings depicting what appears to be a massive battle, is fenced off. However, there is a resident guide who will walk you through on request. It's also one of the few rock-art sites in which an image of a lion is depicted.

One of the best-known and best-loved hikes is the Giant's Cup Trail, a five-day marathon that crosses the mountains from Sani Pass to Bushman's Nek. It is graded as 'moderate', although a few small sections can be quite hard on the muscles. But it's a bit misleading to pick out specific routes: there are hikes and walks to suit all tastes and levels of fitness. Lotheni and Injasuti are popular trout-fishing spots.

Sani Pass

Sani Pass is the only road along the entire, mountainous, 300-kilometre stretch between KwaZulu-Natal and eastern Lesotho. It is 6.5 kilometre long, rises to an altitude of 2 874 metres, and most people get to the top by 4x4. Many of the local Basotho, though, make the journey on their tough little ponies.

To reach the summit you have to cross the international border, so you'll need travel documents. The Sani Pass Hotel is the last privately run oasis before you start the ascent, and it's a pleasant place indeed (large, comfortable, with spacious grounds beautifully designed for outdoor leisure) to return to after what can be a bit of a nerve-wracking excursion. This is a resort built and run in the true, old-fashioned style of the traditional 'Berg hostelries, offering something for the whole family – tennis, bowls, trout fishing, free golf, and some lovely hikes, through indigenous forests, that lead past entrancing waterfalls. There are also a few San rock paintings to be seen along the walks.

As mentioned, the ascent is a popular four-wheel-drive trip, and also something of a challenge for hikers, motorcyclists and mountain bikers. The steep and stony

road twists and winds back on itself as it climbs to ever-dizzying heights. Don't try to negotiate it in the family car (you can't, in any event, cross the border in a sedan vehicle).

A number of tour operators make daily trips up Sani, which has distinct advantages: the excursions take in a visit to a traditional stone-and-thatch Sotho village, where you meet the local Basotho and learn something of their culture. At the top of the pass, too, is a rustic but sturdy little lodge called the Sani Pass Chalet, which offers wonderful views out over the mountains and the lowland plain to the east. The chalet has a small pub and restaurant (light meals), and a couple of rooms if you want to stay over. In winter, this part of the 'Berg is often covered in snow, and it's a real joy to sit around a cosy fire while the weather outside closes in.

Also at the top of the pass, near the lodge, is a vulture restaurant, where carcasses are put out to attract the big raptors that soar above the 'Berg. Star of the show is probably the rare lammergeier, sometimes known as the bearded vulture. These great birds are endangered, victims of the poison that farmers leave out to eradicate jackals and other threats to their livestock.

Splashy Fen

What started as a small get-together of musicians for a few days 'jamming' on Splashy Fen farm, near Bushman's Nek in the Sani area, has grown into one of the country's premier outdoor music festivals. It takes place each year, during April or May, and generally lasts for three days. The festival is something of a showcase for local folk- and blues-bands, but often also features top-name overseas performers. The shows are held in marquees and open-air amphitheatres; among the various supplementaries are an open-air craft market, buskers, jugglers, puppeteers, magicians and fire-eaters to entertain the children.

In true Woodstock-like fashion most people camp in the surrounding hills or down at the river, although there are some excellent guesthouses and bed-and-breakfast establishments in the area.

Some of the Farm's artworks.

ART FROM ARDMORE

Ardmore Guest Farm is home to one of the most respected ceramic studios in the country. The rural studio and gallery had humble beginnings in the beautiful old stone stables of the original Ardmore farm, where women from the surrounding countryside learnt the secrets of ceramics from the owner's wife. They now create their own, very individual works of art, pieces that are internationally sought after. Many are on permanent show at galleries around the world.

The studio is open to the public, and one may pass a pleasant and rewarding few hours wandering around the stables, watching the women turn out their originals. Day visitors enjoy tea and scones outside, under the shade trees, the towering heights of the Drakensberg providing a stunning backdrop. There are also facilities for over-nighters; and the food ranks among the region's best.

TOP *A helicopter sight-seeing trip takes off from Cathedral Peak Hotel.*
ABOVE *The common marsh poker graces the region's swampier areas.*
BELOW *One of the Giant's Castle reserve's chalets.*
BOTTOM RIGHT *Jacob's Ladder Falls, in the Drakensberg's foothills.*

Giant's Castle

This reserve, which perhaps more properly belongs within the central Drakensberg but has its affinities with the southern section, is one of the best locations in southern Africa for viewing San paintings. KZN Wildlife has recently upgraded the popular Giant's Castle Rest Camp and the rock-art site at Main Caves. The camp is set on the grassy plateau in a deep valley below the Giant's Castle massif.

Main Caves are about a 45-minute walk from the camp, and a local guide meets visitors at the entrance (you aren't allowed into the caves on your own). Tours start on the hour every hour

between 09h00 and 15h00, and there is a small entrance fee.

The Giant's Castle reserve was originally proclaimed to protect the region's dwindling herds of eland, and you should keep an eye open for these large, stately antelope during your walk. On the way back from Main Caves you'll come across a site marked Rock 75, the figure carved into the rock by the British Army's 75th regiment, which camped here while blocking the passes in 1874. You'll also see faded San paintings on the rock.

A 'vulture hide' near the rest camp can be visited over weekends from May to September. A maximum of six visitors are taken up to the lookout by vehicle, from where they walk back to camp. Reservations are essential; trips to view the lammergeiers (bearded vultures), Cape vultures, black eagles, jackal buzzards and lanner falcons, to name some of the birds you'll see here, are booked months in advance.

THE CENTRAL 'BERG

The central region is more heavily populated and better developed for tourism than either the southern or northern segments, probably because it is the easiest to get to from the main N3 highway. Moreover, a good tarred road, the R600, will take you from Winterton, one of the two main hubs (the other is Bergville), right into Champagne Valley. The Valley contains an inviting variety of hotels, resorts and self-catering cottages and farm guesthouses, though many visitors choose to head off with their backpacks and sleeping bags to explore and enjoy the stunning wilderness areas accessible from here.

Among the prominent natural features of the central Drakensberg are Cathkin Peak, Monk's Cowl, Champagne Castle, Cathedral Peak and the amazing Ndedema Gorge – to name just a few. Many trails lead into and across the slopes, around the soaring peaks and though fern-filled valleys graced by exquisite waterfalls.

Hikes

Even if you're reluctant to spend nights in the mountains and choose to stay over in one of the comfortable resorts or camp

sites, there are a myriad lovely day walks available to you – not only around the foothills but into the main Drakensberg rampart itself. The Cathedral Peak area alone, for instance, offers eight different hikes from the camp site.

The more intrepid overnight hiker has some 15 caves from which to choose, though you will need a permit before you're allowed to sleep over. Book your cave well beforehand, and share it if bad weather sets in and others need the shelter.

The lovely Rainbow Gorge is an easy walk from Cathedral Peak Hotel, the route taking you through yellowwood forest country. The gorge derives its name

from the rainbows created by the mix of sunshine and the fine spray rising from the many waterfalls that cascade down into the gorge. You will have to cross the river a number of times on your way up in order to circumvent the enormous boulders that crashed down into the gorge hundreds of years ago.

An especially worthwhile three-day hike is that to the Ndedema Gorge, also known as the Valley of the Bushmen and believed to have been one of the very last refuges of the now long-gone San inhabitants. Some of their finest rock paintings are to be found on the sandstone cliffs in and around the gorge. The paths are good, the gradients easy

ABOVE Green and lush during summer, the Drakensberg's peaks, ridges and valleys are often snow-covered in winter.
BELOW Hikers in the high Drakensberg.
BELOW LEFT The mainly nocturnal and solitary serval, usually found in tall grassland near water.

THE WAY OF WHITE WATERS

A fine alternative to hiking the wilderness of the uKhahlamba-Drakensberg Park is one of the white-water trips run by Four Rivers Rafting. These exhilarating excursions are generally organised during the wet summer season (though you'll still be able to raft even if there hasn't been much rain). Rapids are graded one to five; on offer are half-day, full-day, and overnight forays – not as lengthy as the more famous Orange River rafting trips, but just as much fun.

Expeditions on the Thukela (or Tugela) River usually start with a wonderful breakfast under the vines at Thokozisa, a mountain restaurant/coffee house-cum-indigenous nursery-cum-gallery/curio shop near Winterton. From here you're collected and driven to Mambaza, a charming camp on the banks of the river.

There are enough rapids to keep the trip interesting, and enough fast-flowing, flat water to prompt you to welcome the cool-drinks delivered to your canoe, along one of the quieter stretches, by a 'waiter' who is actually a highly experienced 'sweeper' (someone who follows the rafters to ensure that there are no problems). The trip ends a couple of hours later at a camp site, where a sociable and most welcome barbecue and various refreshments are laid on.

TOP *Trout fishing in the Midlands.*
ABOVE *The jackal buzzard, one of many Drakensberg raptors.*
BELOW *The world-renowned Drakensberg Boys' Choir.*

enough. Leopard Cave and Schoongezicht Cave are both popular bases from which to explore the gorge.

The Drakensberg Boys' Choir

There can be few music-lovers who have not heard of the choir, a group of talented youngsters sometimes mentioned in the same breath as their Vienna and Harlem counterparts. The school is tucked away in a surprisingly remote rural community, about 17 kilometres from the R600 crossroads near Winterton. The boys perform for the public every Wednesday afternoon during term time, and their concerts are not to be missed – especially those evenings when they put on a show of foot-stomping, spirit-rousing traditional African music.

Falcon Ridge

Set atop one of the highest points along the R600 route is Falcon Ridge, a display centre for birds of prey that has developed into one of Champagne Valley's most popular venues. Each day its young and enthusiastic owners put on two hour-long shows featuring live demonstrations in which a variety of birds – lanner falcons, peregrine falcons, black eagles, crowned eagles, African hawk eagles among them – are put through their paces. Visitors are both enthralled and informed, gaining a splendid insight into the habits of

some of this high region's most spectacular, and in some case most endangered, avian species.

THE NORTHERN 'BERG
Royal Natal National Park

The Amphitheatre, one of the Drakensberg's most eye-catching landmarks, is a gigantic, crescent-shaped basalt cliff whose sheer rock face rises to more than 2 900 metres in height and measures more than four kilometres across. It is part of the famed Mont-aux-Sources ('Mountain of Springs') massif, on whose plateau summit rise an unusual number of rivers and streams – seven of them to be precise. Among these watercourses are the Elands, which flows north to join the Vaal, the Thukela (or Tugela), which plunges over the Ampitheatre's rim in a 947-metre long series of falls and cascades, one of which drops sheer for 183 metres – which makes it the country's highest and, after the Angel Falls in Venezuela, the world's second highest waterfall.

Prominent among the peaks of the Mont-aux-Sources area are the 3 121-metre high South and Beacon Buttresses, the 3 047-metre Eastern Buttress, and the 3 165-metre northern pinnacle known as The Sentinel.

Nestled at the bottom of the Amphitheatre is the Royal Natal National

Park, an 8 000-hectare expanse of lovely Drakensbeg countryside which has its wild animals, but is perhaps more notable for its bird and plant life – and, of course, for the majestic mountain backdrop and the scenic magnificence of the hills and rolling grasslands, which can be explored on any one of more than two dozen charted walks and hikes. These range from the short and gentle Otto Trail to the 45-kilometre odyssey that takes you up to the Mont-aux-Sources plateau itself (a chain latter helps you over the last small stretch).

There are pleasant hotels and guesthouses in the area. Facilities within the park consist of Mahai and Rugged Glen, two beautiful camping spots. Mahai is a large, open site with big trees dotted about and lovely views of the mountains. It caters for about 400 campers and caravaners. Rugged Glen is much smaller, with just 45 sites. The rivers, with their big pools and cascading waterfalls, are ideal for the occasional, refreshing dip; the watercourses and the two dams invite the discerning trout-fisherman (permits required). Horse trails set out from the stables at Rugged Glen.

And then there's Tendele, one of the most popular hutted camps in the 'Berg, which comprises a luxury lodge and a number of huts, chalets and cottages, each with a stunning view of the Amphitheatre.

Hikes

As mentioned, Royal Natal is something of a paradise for both the hiker and the rambler. Rather special is the six-hour trail that winds its way past the great boulders that line the river to the base of the Ampitheatre.

So too is the two-hour walk from Mahai which takes you to a delightful picnic spot at Glen Wood, and then on to the gorge that connects the wood with a feature known rather appropriately as The Grotto.

TOP Tendele Camp at Royal Natal National Park.
ABOVE A gaudy commodore butterfly.

USEFUL CONTACTS

Howick Publicity Association
Tel: 033 330 5305

Midlands Meander
Cell: 082 803 233 27
Fax: 033 343 3664
mm@futurenet.co.za
www.midlandsmeander.org.za

KZN Wildlife
Tel: 033 845 1000
Fax: 033 845 1001
bookings@rhino.org.za
www.kznwildlife.com

Sani Pass Hotel
Tel: 033 702 1320
Fax: 033 702 0220
sanipasshotel@futurenet.co.za
www.sanipasshotel.co.za

Sani Top Chalets
Tel/Fax: 033 702 1320
drakensberg.info@futurenet.org.za

Splashy Fen
Tel: 031 572 3073
Fax: 031 572 4909
bartf@saol.com
www.splashyfen.co.za

Ardmore Guest Farm
Tel/Fax: 035 468 1314
ardmore@futurenet.co.za
www.ardmore.co.za

Drakensberg Boys' Choir
Tel: 036 448 1557
admin@dbchoir.co.za
www.dbchoir.co.za

Falcon Ridge Bird of Prey Centre
Cell: 082 774 6398

Mountain Meander
Tel: 036 688 1307
Fax: 036 488 1795
www.drakensbergmeander.co.za

Four Rivers Rafting
Tel: 036 422 2259 (Jennifer)
Cell: 083 785 1693
455@telkinsa.net

Rawdons Hotel has charm – and operates its own brewery.

Wetland
Paradise

Maputaland

The low-lying, hot and humid countryside that lies between the Lebombo Mountains in the west and the Indian Ocean in the east is known as Maputaland. It is a magical part of South Africa, regarded as one of the wonders of the natural world for the vast diversity of its ecosystems and, by definition, of its animals and plants. Here you'll find hills, forests, grasslands, great dunes and, most prominently, lakes and lagoons, rivers and their lush floodplains, all hosting their distinctive life forms. Centrepiece of this magical region is the St Lucia wetland complex.

Maputaland

Greater St Lucia Wetland Park, Coastal Forest and Marine Reserve, Mkhuze Game Reserve, Phinda Resource Reserve, Tembe Elephant Park, Ndumo Game Reserve, Ithala Game Reserve

The entire Greater St Lucia Wetland Park, from Mapelane in the south to Kosi Bay in the north, including False Bay Park, Mkhuze Game Reserve and Sodwana Bay National Park, is a World Heritage Site, and is recognised as a Ramsar Wetland Site of international importance. The park is reached via the N2 and its eastward digressions, from both Durban and Johannesburg. It is roughly a six-hour drive from Durban to Kosi Bay, with a number of toll pay-points along the way.

TOP *St Lucia estuary is popular in the holiday season; at other times of the year it can be almost deserted.*
ABOVE *Hippos are among the most visible of St Lucia's mammals, especially in the evenings and early mornings.*
PREVIOUS PAGES *Kosi Bay's limpid estuary, in the far north of KwaZulu-Natal.*

On your way north from Durban on the N2, you'll find that the coastal resorts give way to large expanses of sugar-cane fields and then to exotic pine and eucalyptus plantations. However, it is not all agricultural land. This is where many of KwaZulu-Natal's best-known reserves are located, among them the Greater St Lucia Wetland Park, which includes Sodwana Bay National Park and the coastal forest marine reserves and game sanctuaries of Mkhuze and Phinda, to name a few.

Maputaland, which stretches west to the Lebombo Mountains, east to the coast and north to the Mozambique border, is truly a wilderness wonderland. It lies in the transition area between the tropical and subtropical zones, which accounts for its lavish variety of endemic animals and plants. Large stretches of water such as St Lucia, Bhangazi and Sibaya, and the stunning lake system of Kosi Bay, are

home to crocodiles and hippos. The whole of the Maputaland coastline is a formally protected marine environment.

It is suggested you collect a pamphlet, from the KwaZulu-Natal Wildlife offices, that shows boat launching sites, areas in which you're allowed to fish, and so on.

THE GREATER ST LUCIA WETLAND PARK

The vast park stretches up the east coast for more than 250 000 hectares, and it ecompasses wilderness areas of unsurpassed beauty. Its beaches, ancient breeding grounds of the big sea turtles, are protected by some of the highest coastal dunes in the world.

Mapelane Nature Reserve

Mapelane is a favourite among anglers who come to fish the southern bank of the St Lucia estuary and the Mfolozi River; the area offers a good launch site for ski-boats, and swimming is pretty safe at low tide. There are also trails through the coastal dune forests. The reserve has 10 log cabins, most of them with wonderful sea views, and a caravan and camp site.

St Lucia Village

In contrast to the placid wilderness elsewhere, the village is a busy, rather commercialised resort town. On the left as you enter is a large craft market, run by local women, which is well known for its beadwork and decorative mats.

From here you can take a cruise on the 80-seater *Santa Lucia*. Its passengers will see a wealth of crocs and hippos, and enjoy a wonderful bird life. Two-hour guided launch tours set out three times each day.

Just outside the village, on the road towards Cape Vidal, is the St Lucia Crocodile Centre, where the natural history of the region is illuminated by displays and dioramas. Tours offer an insight into the history and nature of the crocodile and its habitat. The crocs are fed on Saturday afternoons.

Cape Vidal

About 35 kilometres north of St Lucia, along the tarred road is Cape Vidal, a popular fishing venue with an attractive camp site and some self-catering log cabins on the edge of the dune forest. Ski-boaters flock here for sport-fishing and snorkelling, and there is a rewarding four-day guided wilderness trail, through the nearby Tewate Wilderness Area, leading from Lake St Lucia to the sea. Alternatively (or perhaps additionally), two short self-guided trails take you through the forests to Lake Bhangazi. There are fishing camps on the dunes overlooking this lake.

Sodwana Bay

There is no coastal road from Cape Vidal to Sodwana, so you have to backtrack to St Lucia Village and then return to the N2 before continuing north.

Sodwana is one of South Africa's premier diving and sport-fishing venues, and during the season and over weekends the area is packed.

Dive operators set up shop with their large shelters and scuba tanks, and drying wetsuits and picnic baskets seem to be strewn everywhere. It's all very enjoyable even if crowds are not your thing: there is a convivial holiday atmosphere as everyone shares their dive experiences and their fishing stories, and their refreshments. The camp site is one of the biggest along the coast; also on offer are self-catering cottages. During the summer months, KZN Wildlife arranges tours of the region for camp residents. Departure times vary according to the tide.

FOREST AND MARINE RESERVE
Mabibi Coastal Camp

The camp is situated on the coast north of Sodwana Bay and near beautiful Lake Sibaya. It has a lovely setting just a 10-minute stroll (on a raised boardwalk) down the steep coastal forest dune and onto the beach. Each site has its own shade netting, tap and barbecue area, but there is no electricity, so you need to bring firewood. A four-wheel drive is recommended, especially in summer when roads become very sandy. Caravans are discouraged for the same reason.

Lake Sibaya and Baya Camp

Sibaya, the largest freshwater lake in southern Africa, was once connected to the sea but the estuary closed up long ago. Today the crystal-clear waters are home to crocodiles, hippos and a variety of other animals.

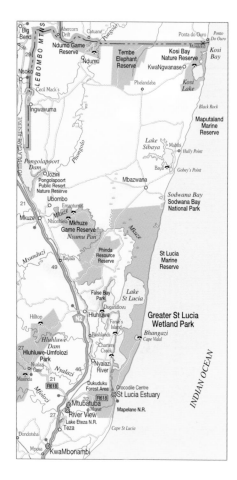

BELOW Each year, in the summer months, loggerhead turtles and their much larger cousins, the leatherbacks, arrive on Maputaland's beaches to lay their eggs.

TOP *The Kumasinga hide at Mkhuze is a fine game-viewing spot, especially in winter when it is dry and many animals, like these nyala, come down to drink.*
ABOVE *Although relatively small, warthogs are formidable opponents, adept at using their tusks when in trouble.*
BELOW *Nsumo Pan in Mkhuze Game Reserve is well known for it's bird life; here thousands of southern white pelicans arrive to fish the waters.*

It is possible to drive around the lake, but a permit must be obtained from the KZN Wildlife offices beforehand. On its southern shores is Baya Camp, a collection of small chalets with a communal lounge/dining area serviced by a fully equipped communal kitchen. The bird life is outstanding – 279 species have been recorded in the immediate area, and there are two lovely viewing hides.

There are also self-guided and conducted walking trails. The presence of crocodiles prohibit swimming in the lake, but there's a pool at the camp.

Rocktail Bay Lodge

There are not, as yet, many luxury beach lodges in South Africa, but Wilderness Safaris operates an extremely pleasant one tucked away in the Maputaland coastal forest midway between Kosi and Sodwana bays. It's run along the same lines as most game lodges – except that the focus is the 40 kilometres of unspoiled beach and coastline rather than on big game. The lodge itself has a wonderful forest tree-house atmosphere.

Masks and fins are available to snorkelling enthusiasts; the birding is outstanding, and, on your walk through the dune forest, there is every chance of seeing smaller antelope species such as duikers. Fishing off the beach is good; saltwater fly-fishing rods are supplied.

The Rocktail Bay coastline is where, during the summer months, many massive loggerhead and leatherback sea turtles make their way onto the beaches to lay their eggs. Lodge guests are able to join staff on their nightly drives along the beach to monitor these ancient marine mammals – a unique experience.

The lodge also has exclusive rights to scuba-dive the 15 beautiful, unspoilt offshore reefs; the fully equipped Mares scuba operation enables guests to view a myriad forms of marine life, including an abundance of reef fish (the magnificent angelfish among them). The ragged-tooth shark breeds in the region. Divers must have the appropriate certificate.

Kosi Bay

Despite its name, Kosi Bay is not a bay at all but the estuary at the end of a sequence of four spacious lakes that stretch for 18 kilometres along the coast, with a splendid peninsula of coastal dune forest looming up between the lakes and the sea.

Hippos, crocodiles and a variety of fish live in the lakes. The locals are excellent fishermen, and for generations have maintained the family fish traps, or fish kraals, that stretch across Lake Makhawulani (or First Lake), which is the one closest to the estuary. These ingenuous wooden pallisade enclosures are carefully positioned in the beautifully clear waters, and can only be visited by boat (ask the locals for permission before doing so) although the fishermen themselves wade across the lake at low tide to empty them. If you do not have your own boat, the two privately owned lodges in the area offer a number of tours. Alternatively, make enquiries at the KZN Wildlife offices.

A camp site is situated on the shore of Lake Nhlange (Third Lake), and there are three self-catering cottages in the area.

The breeding grounds of the loggerhead and leatherback turtles extend all the way up the coast, which can be explored, and the animals viewed, on the tours run by the local folk, by some lodges and by KZN Wildlife. If you're lucky you will see, towards the end of the season, the tiny hatchlings being 'notched' for research purposes at the Banga Neck research station, which is located on the beach side of the peninsula.

Kosi Bay Hiking Trail

For many hiking devotees, this trail stands on a par with the Garden Route's famous Otter Trail. In fact, there are several routes that wind through the varied landscapes, each more spectacular than the one before. The main trail takes four days to complete. The first night is spent at base camp, the second on an 'island' on First Lake (near the fish traps), the third at the beach, the fourth by the magnificent Sihadle River and pan in a small camp.

MKHUZE GAME RESERVE

This fine reserve, situated on the Maputaland coastal plain, at the foot of the Lebombo Mountains and between the Msunduze and mKuzi rivers, is perhaps better known for its birds than for its game – even though it does support many large animals, including white and black rhino, elephant, cheetah, leopard, giraffe and prolific herds of zebra, blue wildebeest, impala, nyala and others.

Some 600 species of bird have been recorded at Mkhuze, and there are six superb hides on the pans and water holes from where you can watch them and the mammals as they come down to drink.

Two of the reserve's most rewarding pans are Nsumo and Nhlonhlela. Nsumo, the larger one, has two elevated bird-viewing hides that provide wonderful vantage points.

Large populations of hippos and crocodiles also wallow in Mkuze's pans. Day and night game-viewing drives can

be booked at Mantuma Main Camp office. The night drives are especially delightful, affording one the rare opportunity to see the nocturnal thick-tailed bushbaby; white-tailed mongoose, porcupine, small spotted genet and sometimes even hyena and leopard.

The spectacular Fig Forest Walk winds through cool glades beneath the dense canopy of the giant sycamore trees.

A variety of accommodation is available to visitors. At the Emshopi entrance gate is a pleasant, reasonably priced caravan park and camp site; other options are Umkumbi Bush Lodge, on the edge of Nhlonhlela Pan, and self-catering bungalows, rest huts and a self-catering tented camp at Mantuma, where there is also a curio shop and swimming pool.

Local folk make and sell traditional craftwork at the cultural village in the KwaJobe section of the reserve.

TOP Exploring the limpid waterways of Kosi Bay by canoe.
ABOVE Crocodiles open their mouths when out of the water to help regulate their body temperature.

THE GREAT FISH DRIVE

During the summer months, the pans of the Kosi Bay area are filled with water, but in winter the levels drop and it is at this time that the villagers get together and, armed with their spears and distinctive *fonya* baskets, catch fish in the fashion of their forefathers. Generally, the group begins at one end of the pan and, working in a long row, 'beat' or chase the fish across to where they are in shallow water. Once a shoal is isolated, the baskets are used to trap them. The hole at the top of the *fonya* basket allows the fisherman to grab or stab his prey with a spear. It is a noisy and happy occasion, and one well worth observing. The fish drive is a seasonal event, though, and the actual timing is unpredictable.

*Luxurious living deep in the bush –
Wilderness Safari's Ndumo Lodge.*

PHINDA RESOURCE RESERVE

The privately owned Phinda reserve adjoins Mkhuze Game Reserve on Mkhuze's southern border, and is made up of seven ecosystems, including savanna, wetlands and the unique sand forests.

Phinda sustains the 'big five' of the animal kingdom – elephant, rhino, lion, leopard and buffalo – along with a variety of antelope and many other life forms. Before the reserve was established, the area was under cultivation but an extensive management and restocking programme has restored it to its original, wild condition – hence the name, Phinda, which means 'the return' in Zulu.

On offer to guests are, among much else, some outstanding game drives with highly trained and knowledgeable rangers. Extras such as bush walks and birding safaris are optional, and there are also not-to-be-missed early morning and 'sundowner' boat trips on the Mzinene River, excursions on which you can see, among other things, a wealth of water birds. Phinda also lays on off-the-reserve trips in the lodge's private aircraft (which take you over the spectacular Maputaland wilderness); scuba safaris to nearby Sodwana Bay, and deep-sea fishing expeditions.

Phinda is almost as famous for the luxury of its accommodation, and the service lavished on guests, as it is for its game. There are four lodges, two in the north of the reserve and two in the south. Forest Lodge, situated in a magnificent stand of torchwood trees, consists of 16 stilted, glass-and-wood chalets that appear to float just off the ground.

Vlei Lodge, also in the northern section, has more of an East African look (glass, teak and thatch), each unit graced by its own private plunge pool and deck. As their names suggest, Mountain and Rock lodges, in the south, are in the hillier terrain, and are appropriately designed. The small, exclusive Rock Lodge is beautifully built – of roughly hewn stone, and adobe walls – and its suites, again, have their own plunge pools and decks. The latter look out across the reserve to the magnificent Leopard Rock.

TEMBE ELEPHANT PARK

As its name suggests, this sanctuary is known for its wild elephant population. In fact it is home to KwaZulu-Natal's largest endemic herd.

At one time, before fences were erected between Mozambique and South Africa, these animals ranged freely and seasonally between Maputaland and its northern neighbour. A small herd still remains on the other side of the barrier, in the Maputo Elephant Park.

Tembe, the province's third largest game reserve, consists predominantly of sand-forest vegetation, which sometimes makes the animals hard to spot. Apart from the elephant, the park sustains three of the other big five; only lion are missing. On your game drive you may come across buffalo, and both white and, less often, black rhino. There are also giraffe, kudu and nyala. The pans are full of hippos, and if you're really lucky you might see one of South Africa's smallest antelope, the tiny suni, which makes its home in the sand forest. The birding, particularly at the water holes, is excellent.

Unless you are booked into Tembe Safari Camp, the only overnight accommodation, you will be allowed in only if you have a day permit, and these are limited. So make enquiries through KwaZulu-Natal Wildlife offices before you set off for the park. The camp is tucked away in the sand forest and has a small swimming pool – a real bonus during the sweltering late spring and summer months. Day and night drives are on offer.

NDUMO GAME RESERVE

Ndumo is renowned as one of the subcontinent's premier birding spots. There are a number of excellent pans that fill up during the rainy summer season, drawing birds in their thousands. Here you can listen to the distinctive call of the African fish eagle; see such rare species as Pel's fishing owl; view at leisure, from the hides overlooking the pans, a myriad other water birds. The summer migrants arrive between October and April, when the pans – the Banzi and Nyamithi among them – fill with life-giving water.

But Ndumo is not just about birds. You'll also see black and white rhino, giraffe, suni, bushbuck, impala and, in the swampy floodplain, the occasional buffalo. Game drives are available, as is reasonably priced accommodation in a hutted camp of good, old-fashioned rondavels. An alternative is the more expensive Ndumo Wilderness Camp, run by Wilderness Safaris – a luxurious, East African-style tented venue with decks overlooking Banzi Pan. On offer are boat trips on the pan's waterways, when you can observe the game while enjoying a sundowner. A feature of the trip is the 'fish ladder', a weir at the bottom of which lie huge crocodiles with their mouths open, waiting for fish to come tumbling down the waterfall and straight into their gaping jaws!

ITHALA GAME RESERVE

Situated in the north of KwaZulu-Natal, overlooking the Pongola River Valley,

fairly close to the Mozambique border, Ithala rates as one of the most scenic of the reserves. It is known for its geological diversity and excellent game-viewing. Parts of the area are reclaimed farmland, others are grassland and rugged mountainous thornveld, all of which provide habitats for a wide variety of animals. Here you will almost certainly see white rhino, together with elephant and other plains animals.

The main camp, Ntshwondwe, is backed by cliffs that host a variety of raptors, and to sit on one's veranda and watch them soar in the sky above is delight indeed. Wild fig, acacia and cassonia trees surround the camp, which has a restaurant and swimming pool.

The camp site is excellent. Accommodation is also offered in a number of more private bush lodges or camps in the reserve.

TOP One of the all-time great bush drives must surely be that around Ndumo's Nyamithi Pan with it's fever trees, hippos, crocodiles and stunning bird life.
ABOVE Guests at Ndumo Lodge stop to have a look at one of the many Nile crocodiles that occur in Nyamithi pan.
BELOW The Pongola River, Ithala's northern boundary.
OPPOSITE Many of Tembe's elephants have impressive ivory, unlike this one walking past a schotia tree.

Zulu Kingdom

Zululand and the Battlefields

Inland from Durban is handsome Pietermaritzburg, a fine base from which to explore KwaZulu-Natal's proud and splendid Zulu heritage – and the historic battlefields on which, for close on a century, Zulu, Boer and Briton competed bitterly for possession of the land. The Battlefields Route takes you through a sometimes spectacular, always beautiful countryside that flatters to deceive, for, although you wouldn't think so to look at them, these rolling hills and rivers and gentle grasslands once served as the blood-soaked cockpit of southern Africa.

Zululand and the Battlefields

Pietermaritzburg, The Battlefield Sites, Simunye Pioneer Village, Hluhluwe-Umfolozi Park, Hluhluwe Village, Mtunzini, Shakaland

The countryside to the north of the Tugela River is known as Zululand, a historic region without clear borders but nevertheless distinctive, defined by its proud past and the unique cultural tapestry it embraces. The principal routes are the N2 (coastal) and N3 (inland through Pietermaritzburg); good roads branch off to the east and west respectively.

PIETERMARITZBURG

Pietermaritzburg has functioned as the provincial capital, but now shares that status with historic Ulundi, some 80 kilometres to the northwest of Durban.

The settlement was originally established as a Boer outpost, but became a British military garrison in 1843. Today, the city still has many landmarks that evoke its colonial past, including some beautiful examples of Victorian and Edwardian, mainly red-brick, architecture. Among buildings of note are the City Hall and the nearby Tatham Art Gallery, which once functioned as the Supreme Court. The Tatham is now a fine exhibition venue with an outstanding permanent collection of works by South African artists. It also has an extensive display of beadwork, basketry and other traditional crafts. Its small upstairs restaurant and coffee shop overlook the busy city streets.

Not so commendable, perhaps, is Publicity House with its infamous tower, whose bell, during the years of apartheid, was used to ring the nine o'clock curfew, at which time all black people had to be off the streets.

Weenen Game Reserve

To get to Weenen, take the R103 off the N3 either at Estcourt or Colenso, and turn onto the R74. The 6 500-hectare reserve is small by South African standards, but is highly valued as one of the few formally protected stretches of valley bushveld in the country.

This is not 'big five' country, but it does support rhino, and the birding is excellent (279 recorded species). Game drives, night drives, guided and self-guided trails and well-placed hides and water holes are all on offer. Unlike many other small game sanctuaries, Weenen has a wonderful little caravan and camp site just inside the entrance. A tented camp and a cottage are also available. African curios are on sale at the little craft centre just outside the camp.

THE BATTLEFIELD SITES
The Talana Museum

This museum, on the fringes of Dundee, is among the country's most impressive. It's built on the site of the Battle of Talana, the opening engagement of the Anglo-Boer War. Nine separate buildings, two of which were used by the British as field dressing rooms during the battle, house displays telling the story of the region from the time of the San hunter-gatherers up to the Anglo-Boer War. An especially interesting section is that devoted to the extermination of the

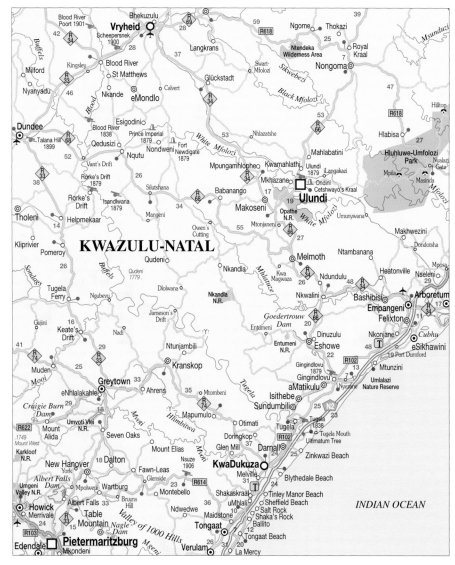

FAR LEFT Zulu dancing – a flamboyant and vibrant tradition.
LEFT Dave Rattray brings the Battle of Isandlwana alive for his guests.
BOTTOM LEFT The Blood River Monument near Vryheid, where the Boers and Zulus fought the decisive battle (1838).
OPPOSITE, ABOVE A stark reminder of Isandlwana, one of South Africa's bloodiest confrontations (1879).
OPPOSITE, BOTTOM Prince Galenja Biyela wears leopard skins befitting of his senior status in the Zulu community.
PREVIOUS PAGES Sunrise over Hluhluwe-Umfolozi Park paints the Black Umfolozi River orange as another day in Africa's oldest game reserve dawns

cannibals who lived in the nearby Biggarsberg in the early 1900s. A restored miner's wood-and-iron cottage has been transformed into a small but rather good restaurant.

Tours of the museum should be booked in advance. Alternatively, visitors may just wander around on their own.

Blood River Monument

The sixteenth of December is a public holiday in South Africa. It's known as The Day of Reconciliation, but has been observed under a number of other names – 'Dingane's Day', 'The Day of the Covenant', 'The Day of the Vow', the last two commemorating a pledge made by the eastern Voortrekkers (Boers) that, if God should grant them victory over the Zulu nation, they would forever after observe the date as a day of thanksgiving.

In the early months of 1838, Voortrekker leader Piet Retief and some 100 members of his group were killed on the orders of the Zulu king, Dingane, at his capital, uMgungundlovu, and as a consequence of this and other bloody confrontations, the two sides squared up to each other for the final showdown at the Ncome River, a tributary of the Thukela. It was an unequal match – raw courage proved no match for the muskets and laagered discipline of the invaders – and the river ran with the blood of dead warriors. Boer casualties were minimal.

BASES FOR THE BATTLEFIELDS

The battle sites of Isandlwana and Rorke's Drift have triggered a lifelong passion in David Rattray, owner of Fugitive's Drift Lodge. His guests – men and women alike – seldom return from a tour with dry eyes. David is a world authority on the battles, and the tour is a memorable experience. It begins either at breakfast or dinner, followed by a morning or evening walkabout over one of the two sites, during which a great deal of information is imparted.

The nearby Isandlwana Lodge is also a good place at which to base yourself for exploring these two sites, or indeed when touring the battlefields in general. The luxury lodge is set dramatically atop iNyoni Rocks, the very cliffs from which Zulu commanders directed the battle. The lodge offers magnificent views, much the same as the commanders would have had, over the battlefield. The lodge's enormous wooden pillars, salvaged from an early shipyard and built into the natural stone, glass and thatch structure, each bear the name of one of the Zulu generals.

ABOVE Anglo-Zulu War monuments at Fugitive's Drift.
BELOW Zulu dancing at Simunye Lodge begins in the early evening, and often continues until very late into the night.

Today, a monument of 64 bronze ox wagons, precisely arranged on the empty veld in the original laager formation, marks the battleground. It is an eerie, oddly moving place.

Isandlwana and Rorke's Drift

The battles of Isandlwana and Rorke's Drift are the two best-known of the Anglo-Zulu War of 1879. The strange Sphinx-like Isandlwana mountain, at the foot of which the former was fought, has a strange, sad, desolate air about it at certain times of the day.

On 17 January 1879, a Zulu army of about 20 000 soldiers began their march from King Cetshwayo's capital at Ondini to confront the British army encamped at Isandlwana. The attack, on 22 January, was a total surprise, and the British and their local allies were slaughtered almost to a man in what proved to be one of the worst defeats suffered by Queen Victoria's armies during the whole of her long reign. The victors then moved on to invade the small mission station and military outpost at Rorke's Drift. However, the 100 or so defenders, warned by survivors from Isandlwana, barricaded themselves in and managed to withstand assault after assault through the long hours. Eleven Victoria Crosses were subsequently awarded, some of them posthumously, largely to lift the morale of both the troops and the British public at home.

Self-guided trails lead you around both battle sites, and a helpful pamphlet is available from the Rorke's Drift Museum, but to make these sites come alive you really need a knowledgeable historian or a good guide to accompany you. Across the road from the museum is an art and craft centre founded by the local mission.

Ondini

Ulundi is situated just north of what was the military capital of the once powerful Zulu nation, Ondini. In July of 1879, the Zulu army was finally crushed when the British attacked the great encampment, after which they burnt it to the ground.

In Zulu tradition, the re-use of royal land is restricted, so until fairly recently the battle site, centre of which was King Cetshwayo's royal kraal, had remained virtually untouched since its destruction. However, restoration of the massive military complex has begun, and many of the traditional beehive homesteads have reappeared (the huts and artefacts were of natural materials, so little escaped the flames). One item that did survive is a large rock on which the king would sit while he was being bathed, and from where he could see out over the surrounding hills.

The re-creation project involves more than just the kraal and the royal homestead. A museum and interpretative centre has been added, together with a

large statue of Cetshwayo. Guides are available to take you around both the kraal site and the museum, which has some fascinating exhibits depicting the traditional Zulu way of life. There are also displays that help tell the British story of the battle.

SIMUNYE ZULU LODGE

As cultural villages go, Simunye, just outside the town of Melmoth, rates as one of the best. Smaller than the busy, rather more commercialised Shakaland (see further on), Simunye really does offer authenticity – even though the spectacular accommodation adjacent to the actual village perhaps evokes African fantasy rather than Zulu tradition. Visitors ride down into the valley on horseback or in an old wagon, both preferable to a four-wheel-drive vehicle (the road is bad). It may sound quite uncomfortable and slow in the wagon, but it really sets the mood for this novel excursion.

On arrival you are met by a torch-bearing Zulu *impi* (miltary force). There is no electricity – candles or hurricane lamps provide the light, and contribute to the wonderful African ambience. The Zulu village is set across the river; a tour will include the all-important cattle kraal, the tasting of traditional Zulu beer, and spear-throwing and bead-making demonstrations. But it is almost worth visiting Simunye for the luxury of its accommodation alone. The units – among them rooms en suite, some with individual bathrooms – are set against a cliff face and built of rough-hewn rock, stone and thatch. Moreover, if there are any traditional celebrations – weddings, coming-of-age ceremonies and so on – scheduled for the surrounding area during your visit, there is every chance you will be invited to see the real thing.

HLUHLUWE-UMFOLOZI PARK

Located some 250 kilometres from Durban, the Hluhluwe-Umfolozi is one of the country's premier provincial game reserves and, at 96 000 hectares, one of its largest. It is a 'big five' sanctuary, but there's a lot more to see than lion, leopard, elephant, buffalo and rhino. In

residence are many plains animals, among them wildebeest and zebra, kudu, the shaggy-coated nyala, bushbuck, waterbuck and baboon. More than 425 species of bird have been recorded in the area, including the acrobatic bateleur and the white-backed vulture. It is also haven to cheetah, and, most excitingly, the endangered African wild dog.

It was from this reserve that Operation Rhino, a project that saved the white rhino from extinction, was launched in the early 1960s to become one of conservation's truly great success stories. In the Umfolozi section of the park are some of the best wilderness trails you'll find anywhere: hikers eat around a campfire, and sleep under the stars, and

TOP AND ABOVE Arguably one of the most beautiful of South Africa's parks, the Hluhluwe-Umfolozi is home to the subcontinent's largest population of the endangered white rhino.

TOP AND ABOVE *Shakaland – one of the most spectacular of cultural villages.* BELOW *Young Zulu women at DumaZulu Kraal near Hluhluwe demonstrate their bead-making skills.*

explore an area that supports an almost unmatched array of animals. Armed rangers accompany the group.

There is a short, weekend trail, a four-night wilderness hike, and a third, somewhat primitive route designed for the hardcore enthusiast.

On offer is a range of accommodation to suit all tastes and budgets – exclusive lodges, camp sites, tented camps and bush camps. The Hluhluwe section has bush lodges as well as a number of self-catering and other chalets at its big Hilltop Camp, which is situated in a prime spot on the edge of a steep, forested slope. Hilltop's guests enjoy breathtaking views over the hills of Zululand. The camp restaurant is excellent.

HLUHLUWE VILLAGE
DumaZulu Kraal
Tours of this cultural village, 10 kilometres south of Hluhluwe, are conducted daily by one of a team of trained and highly knowledegable guides. Kraal residents carry out an ongoing variety of age-old routines, among them the making of clay pots, baskets, beadwork, spears and shields. One can also visit a local sangoma, or traditional healer.

Among other attractions are a restaurant, connected to the village by a walkway, that serves traditional food (a delicious buffet, as well as light snacks); shebeen (Zulu bar), a curio shop; and a snake-pit and crocodile-park complex containing 40 snake species and

subspecies from all over the world. The resident herpetologist conducts daily demonstrations.

One may overnight at DumaZulu Lodge, whose units, in keeping with African tradition, are arranged in two circular formations. The exterior of each hut has been decorated to represent the country's various cultures (they range from the Xhosa of the south to the Venda of the north).

Crafts on Show
Hluhluwe Village is host to the Ilala Weavers' shop, which sells traditional arts and crafts mainly of local Zulu origin. The place is packed with beautiful craftwork, the quality of which is unusually high. The shop functions along the lines of a cottage-industry cooperative; locals are encouraged and trained to improve skills they already have as well as learn new ones; and they turn out a nice range of contemporary items – carved wooden salad servers, painted enamelware, basketware, lampshades, woven briefcases, fashion ware and so on – as well as traditional products. After browsing, one can enjoy a good meal at the restaurant, which is decorated with many of the handmade items that can be found in the shop.

MTUNZINI
Mtunzini, a small coastal village 30 kilometres south of Richards Bay, is famous for its large raffia-palm plantation. Here, the rare and magnificent palms, some of them 23 metres tall, are at more-or-less the southernmost limit of their distribution, and the stand has been declared a national monument. The equally rare palmnut vulture, which you will see if you're lucky, is dependent on these trees, and Egyptian fruit bats roost in the canopy. Facilities include a small, shady picnic area and a wooden walkway through the grove.

The area also has a long stretch of unspoiled beach, more popular for fishing than for swimming, and a pretty lagoon where you can enjoy all manner of watersports. There is an interesting trail, which children love, along a boardwalk: it winds its way through the mangroves near the mouth of the lagoon.

SHAKALAND

This complex, off the R66 near Eshowe, is one of the busiest and most popular cultural and historical centres in the country, a 'living' Zulu village that simply must be included in your itinerary. You visit people in their 'homes', and watch as they brew beer and make traditional pottery, beadwork and spears, and perhaps try your hand at spear-throwing and stick-fighting. A sangoma, is also there to reveal the secrets of his trade.

The place was originally built as the set for the acclaimed television series *Shaka Zulu*, and was later converted.

Most visitors come only for a morning or afternoon tour, but others enjoy a night in one of the reconstructed beehive homes, all of which are now equipped with modern conveniences. Day-visitor tours around the village are conducted twice a day. For overnighters, the events culminate with highly entertaining after-dinner demonstrations of traditional African dancing.

The restaurant menu is an interesting combination of authentic Zulu and Western dishes; items include barbecued meat or chicken, pumpkin, spinach and *phuthu* (maize meal). There is a small curio shop at the entrance.

TOP On the Umfolozi Wilderness Trail – through an area with no vehicle access.
ABOVE A traffic jam with a difference in Hluhluwe-Umfolozi Park.

USEFUL CONTACTS

Pietermaritzburg Tourism
Tel: 033 345 1348
Fax: 033 394 3535
info@pmbtourism.co.za
www.pmbtourism.co.za

Hilltop Camp's fully equipped chalets.

KZN Wildlife
Tel: 033 845 1000
Fax: 033 845 1001
bookings@kznwildlife.com
www.kznwildlife.com

Battlefields Route information
Cell: 082 802 1643
Fax: 034 981 0176
route@battlefields.org.za
www.battlefields.kzn.org.za

KwaZulu Monuments Council and Heritage Trust
Tel: 035 870 2050
Fax: 035 870 2054
amafahq@mweb.co.za

Talana Museum
Tel: 034 212 2654
Fax: 034 212 2376
info@talana.co.za
www.talana.co.za

Fugitive's Drift Lodge
Tel: 034 642 1843 or 271 8051
Fax: 034 271 8053
fugdrift@trustnet.co.za
www.fugitives-drift-lodge.com

Simunye Zulu Lodge
Tel: 035 450 3111
Fax: 035 450 2534
www.proteahotels.com/hotel/
    hotel.asp?h=sa_kn08

Shakaland
Tel: 035 460 0912
Fax: 035 460 0824
res@shakaland.com
www.shakaland.com

Mtunzini Tourist Information
Tel/Fax: 035 340 1471
ncass@saol.com
www.mtunzini.co.za

Simunye Zulu Lodge.

Rorke's Drift Museum
Tel: 034 642 1687

Ilala Weavers
Tel: 035 562 0630/1
Fax: 035 562 0361
ilala@iafrica.com
www.ilala.co.za

DumaZulu Kraal
Tel/Fax: 035 562 2260
dumazulu@iafrica.com
www.goodersonleisure.com

Bays of Plenty

The Eastern Cape Coast and Hinterland

*T*ravellers who drive straight through the Eastern Cape from the Garden Route to Durban, hardly stopping along the way, miss out on a magical experience: this stretch of the coast and its hinterland has some of South Africa's most inviting beaches, its most dramatic seascapes, its most spectacular scenery, its most fascinating cultural heritage. Port Elizabeth, Grahamstown and East London are the principal urban centres; the elephants of the Addo park and the unspoilt beauty of the famed Wild Coast are arguably the main attractions.

The Eastern Cape Coast and Hinterland

Cape St Francis and Jeffreys Bay, Port Elizabeth, Shamwari, Addo Elephant National Park, Grahamstown, East London, The Wild Coast, Port St Johns, Umtata

The main route east from the lovely St Francis Bay area is the N2 highway, which runs inland for much of the way, but plenty of secondary roads, some of them gravelled, lead down to the coast, and they are well worth exploring – many lead to charming, beach-fringed bays, secluded resorts and pretty little seaside hamlets.

TOP Port Elizabeth's Boardwalk casino and entertainment complex glitters at night.
ABOVE There is much more to Bay World than fishes and dolphins; this dinosaur exhibit takes you back in time.
OPPOSITE, TOP Viewing elephants at the Shamwari reserve.
OPPOSITE, BOTTOM One of three rescued leopard cubs at Shamwari.
PREVIOUS PAGES Coffee Bay typifies the Wild Coast's mix of sandy bays and cliffs that plunge into the Indian Ocean.

CAPE ST FRANCIS AND JEFFREYS BAY

St Francis Bay and Jeffreys Bay are legendary coastal resorts, their reputation resting largely on their superlative surfing waves. Competitive surfers from all over the world make the pilgrimage to J-Bay – as Jeffreys is affectionately known – to challenge the incredible supertubes.

The surf, however, is almost incidental to the hundreds of ordinary families who spend their holidays swimming, snorkelling and generally enjoying the Jeffreys Bay area's more than 30 kilometres of pristine beaches. The village of St Francis Bay, just to the east, used to cater for much the same sort of clientele, but since the development of the man-made marina, it has become rather more upmarket. Nearby Port St Francis is a working harbour and worth a visit: it has its amenities, and it's fun to watch the calamari fleet and the yachts coming in to dock in the evenings, after a hard day at sea. The angling all along this coastline is

hugely rewarding, and so is the marine life: dolphins play in the waves, whales calve and give birth just offshore in the safety of the bays, and there are more than 400 different types of seashell to be found along the beaches. Those interested in the latter can view a wonderful display in the small Jeffreys Bay Shell Museum.

PORT ELIZABETH

Almost 100 kilometres to the east of Jeffreys, around the great sweep of St Francis Bay, is Port Elizabeth, the region's fast-beating industrial heart, its major seaport, and a tourist destination that enjoys growing popularity. It has some of the country's most spacious and safest swimming beaches, among them King's, Humewood, Hobie, Pollok, Brighton, Bluewater Bay, St George's Strand and Wells Estate – a necklace of white sands that stretches for some 40 kilometres around Algoa Bay.

Port Elizabeth is informally known as the 'Windy City', and for good reason: the strong offshore breezes (and the occasional big wind) that often blow are generous to the yachting and windsurfing fraternity. The Swartkops River, near Brighton Beach, is navigable for 18 kilometres upstream, making it something of a watersports playground;. Amsterdamhoek, at the river mouth, has two yacht clubs. The soft corals, the gullies and shipwrecks – such as the *Pati* wreck on Thunderbolt Reef, and the scuttled SAS *Harlem* – attract scuba divers from afar.

Bay Charters runs cruises around the harbour, introducing its clients to the great southern right whales that sport in the offshore waters, the dolphins, Cape fur seals, the myriad sea birds and the delightful (though now endangered) African penguins. On the city beachfront is the Bayworld oceanarium, part of a museum complex famed for its dolphin show, its snake park, tropical house and its fascinating dinosaur display. The museum also encompasses an observatory, which is open to the public on the first and third Wednesday of each month, weather permitting. On offer is a 'guided talk' conducted by members of the PE People's Observatory, who tell you all about the southern night sky.

SHAMWARI

This luxurious, privately owned and run safari reserve covers 18 000 hectares of pleasant, malaria-free wilderness countryside about 45 minutes by road from Port Elizabeth (in the general direction of Grahamstown). Its biggest drawcards are probably the 'big five' of the animal kingdom – lion, leopard, elephant, rhino, buffalo – which, together with a splendid array of other wildlife species, you can see on your game drive. The reserve is blessed, perhaps uniquely so, with five different ecosystems and thus with an unusual variety of life forms.

Guests at Shamwari have a choice of half-a-dozen lodges, the biggest of them Long Lee Manor, originally built in 1910 and since upgraded along graceful British colonial lines. Other lodges are beautifully restored 1820 British settler homesteads.

At Khaya Lendaba, Shamwari's African cultural village, visitors gain an insight into Xhosa lifestyles, traditions and customs through, among other things, music and dance. Next to the village is the Shamwari–Born Free Foundation centre, a rehabilitation sanctuary for animals that have been rescued from captivity.

Day-visitors are welcome at Shamwari, the tour encompassing the cultural village, the Born Free Foundation, and a three-hour game drive.

ADDO ELEPHANT NATIONAL PARK

The Addo park is one of South Africa's most notable conservation success stories. The great herds of Cape elephant were shot out to the brink of extinction during

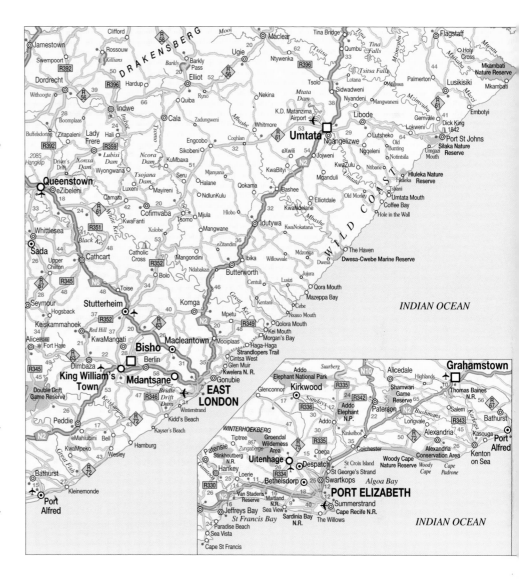

the 19th century, both by the farmers who had settled the land and by hunters in quest of ivory, and by 1920 the eastern Cape elephant population had dwindled to a mere 11 animals. The park was proclaimed in 1931 to protect the pitiful survivors; today it supports more than 350 elephants. In addition, the park has preserved the last natural wild population of Cape buffalo.

Addo is 72 kilometres northeast of Port Elizabeth, near the Zuurberg range in the Sundays River Valley. The park's environment is quite different from most other game sanctuaries in the country: it covers a splendid expanse of gently rolling hills consisting predominantly of Valley Bushveld vegetation – the dense Addo bush is characterised by an abundance of the tough, woody spekboom, a favourite food source for the elephant. There are ambitious plans

ABOVE Safe fun in the sun is what East London's Nahoon River and Beach is all about.
BELOW Gorah Elephant Camp, built around a restored colonial homestead in Addo Park, offers luxury tented suites, superb dining and excellent game-viewing.
BOTTOM The lively National Festival of the Arts takes place in Grahamstown, usually in July each year.

to expand the park both in terms of its size and its overall purpose, a process that started with the incorporation of the former, mountainous Zuurberg National Park to the north.

Although there are no lion in Addo, it does sustain buffalo, kudu, eland, bushbuck, red hartebeest, common duiker, grysbok and a small number of black rhino, together with around 185 species of birds. There is an excellent bird-watching hide at a small dam near the restaurant at the main camp.

One can drive through the park in one's own vehicle between sunrise and sunset, or book a night or day game drive (through the main office). The wildlife can also be observed from the park's cottages and chalets, which overlook a large, illuminated water hole, and on one or other of the two walking trails. Addo's elephants are much more relaxed than those in other game reserves around the country, probably because there hasn't been any culling. This means that even breeding herds with newborn calves are confident enough to allow visitors to approach within a few metres.

Guests have a variety of accommodation options from which to choose, ranging from self-catering units to camping and caravan sites, all reasonably priced. Apart from the restaurant, there is a swimming pool and tennis court for overnighters, and a pretty picnic site for day visitors.

Gorah Elephant Camp

Located within Addo, this is the first such concession granted to private enterprise within a national park, a luxurious, colonial-safari venue of large tents set on a gentle hillside – plus a very impressive main lodge. The latter is an exquisitely restored and furnished 19th-century farmhouse with a wide veranda, where meals are served under the stars. There's a small dam in front of the house, and to sit on the veranda on your comfortable couch, sipping a sundowner and watching the elephants stroll past on their way to the water, is delight indeed.

So sustaining is the spekboem vegetation that Addo is able to support an elephant population that is about three times denser than that of any other reserve in Africa, so it is highly unlikely that you won't see the animals on your game drive. Rangers take guests out, on both early morning and late evening/night excursions, in luxury four-by-fours well stocked with snacks, cool-drinks and excellent coffee.

GRAHAMSTOWN
The Grahamstown Festival

Grahamstown is a small university city situated more or less halfway between Port Elizabeth and East London. Apart from the town's numerous churches (it's informally known as the 'City of Saints'), many good schools and the university, its major claim to fame is the role it plays as host to the annual National Festival of the Arts, generally regarded as the premier cultural event on the African continent and one of the largest and most lively in the world. It runs for about 10 days, usually during early July.

The main programme features a wide selection of disciplines, including drama, just about every form of dance you can think of, music, the visual arts, cabaret, a book fair, film festivals and bustling open-air craft markets. There are also student drama and winter school lectures, and an excellent Fringe Festival, which reflects what is happening on the grass-roots arts scene. Every possible venue is used, from fully equipped, modern theatres to Gothic chapels, old gaols and school halls, and the streets are alive with impromptu entertainment of every sort.

EAST LONDON

East London is one of South Africa's 'big five' harbour cities – although it is unique among them in that it's a river port – and much of the place has developed around the docks and its activities. And it is probably the most convenient large town from which to begin your trip along the Wild Coast (see below), and into the Eastern Cape interior.

The beaches are broad, ideal for the bather, surfer and lazer in the sun, and there is some excellent offshore wreck diving to be enjoyed. Since 1847, more than 150 ships have come to grief within five miles of the city. The only visible wreck, though, is the *Orient*, which can be seen from Orient Beach. The local diving association will organise exploratory trips to some of the sites, but you do need an official scuba-diving certificate in order to join in.

THE WILD COAST

This magnificent seaboard stretches about 280 kilometres from Haga Haga, 90 kilometres northeast of East London, to Port Edward on the border of the Eastern Cape and KwaZulu-Natal. Along the coast there are thick indigenous forests, grassy hills that roll down towards the beaches, secluded little coves, sweeping estuaries teeming with fish, and majestic waterfalls crashing down over jagged rocky ledges into rivers and the sea. It is possible to hike along almost the entire length of the Wild Coast. Some superb 4x4 and mountain-biking trails are run by African Adventures; of special note is the Coastal Esikhaleni route from East London to Coffee Bay. Hiking trails include the following:

Strandloper Trail

The route, which takes five days to complete, starts at Kei Mouth and ends at the boardwalk at Gonubie, just outside East London.

This wonderful coastal trail – most of which leads you through Eastern Cape nature reserve land – makes its way past stunning little coves, long white beaches with not another soul in sight, shipwrecks, tall cliffs and wave platforms. The longest day's stretch is a comfortable 4.5-kilometre walk, mostly along a rocky coastline with narrow intertidal beaches. Overnight accommodation is in rustic rondavels or huts; trailists take their own food, sleeping bags and small cookers.

Wild Coast Hotel Meander

Rather than lug a heavy backpack, filled with all your sleeping and cooking equipment, for miles up the coast, an inviting alternative is the Hotel Meander. On this, you need carry just a day-pack because nights are spent in comfort at one or other of the well-known old Wild Coast family hotels. The 55-kilometre, five-night six-day excursion is available only out of season, when the hotels are not fully booked.

ABOVE The lovely Mgawa Falls, near Lusikisiki, are not very well known but are well worth a visit.
BELOW Morgan's Bay, just south of the Kei River mouth, is a sleepy, and very relaxing, little holiday destination.

*TOP The undulating hills of the Eastern
Cape coastal region.
ABOVE Amakweta (Xhosa initiates) at their
graduation ceremony. After the rituals the
initiates are considered to be men, and are
permitted to marry.
BELOW Cape cormorants are excellent at
catching fish, but need to dry out from time
to time.*

Trailists may arrange to be collected
in East London and driven to Kob Inn,
where they spend their first night. The
second is at Mazeppa Bay Hotel, the
third at Wavecrest (notable, among other
things, for its crowned cranes), the fourth
at Trennery's, and the final one at the
wonderful old Morgan's Bay Hotel.

The trail is pleasantly varied,
incorporating river crossings (one on a
pontoon), beach walks and hiking over
the stunning headlands that overlook the
sea. There is ample opportunity to bathe
in the usually warm waters of the Indian
Ocean, and it's suggested you take along
a small 'telescope' fishing rod: there are
excellent angling opportunities in the
gullies and estuaries. Picnic lunches are
provided by individual hotels.

Dwesa-Cwebe Wildlife Reserve and Marine Sanctuary

Dwesa and Cwebe are situated on
either side of the mangrove-lined Mbashe
River. Dwesa is the slightly larger of the
two sections (3 900 hectares); Cwebe lies
to the north and is about 2 140 hectares
in extent.

Three smaller rivers also run through
the reserve, spilling out into the ocean
along the reserve boundary. The Dwesa-
Cwebe is well endowed with evergreen
forest and water, so the birding is quite
excellent. Look out for mangrove
kingfishers, tiny green twinspots, Knysna
woodpeckers and the shy and beautiful
Narina trogon. The beaches run the
length of the reserve – beautiful, long

stretches of white sand broken by rocky
outcrops; secluded little bays invite the
swimmer, sunbather, snorkeller and the
shell collector. Rock pools are home to
a fine variety of east-coast marine
creatures. Paths and trails wind through
the towering forests, over streams and
up to the top of the grassy Kobole Point,
from where you enjoy a stunning view
out across the sea. On a good day you
can see dolphins, whales and sometimes
even turtles from this vantage spot. Sheer
cliffs drop dramatically from the Point
into the ocean.

Accommodation at Dwesa is in self-
catering stilted wooden chalets set snugly
in the forest, or at a well laid-out camp-
site at the edge of the forest near the
Ingomana River, about 40 metres from
the beach. Keep all your food locked up,
and close the tent-flap or the windows of
your hut when you go out: the monkeys
are clever little thieves.

The Haven, the well-known family
hotel situated in the Cwebe section, can
be accessed from the N2 south of Umtata.
Take the Elliotdale turnoff towards the
coast: from here, it's about 65 kilometres
along a gravel road. At the time of
writing the hotel was temporarily closed
but not, hopefully, for long.

Hole in the Wall and Coffee Bay

A few kilometres south of Coffee Bay
stands a huge detached cliff with a giant
opening carved through its centre by
centuries of wave action. It is possible,
when the tide is very low, to wade or
even walk out to the Hole in the Wall,
but take care – the tide and current whirl
around the outcrop and the channel can
be quite dangerous.

The thunderous waves that crash
through the hole at high tide is a sight
and sound not easily forgotten.

For visitors, there used to be nothing
more than a small holiday cottage
settlement in the vicinity, but now the
place has its hotel, and timeshare
accommodation is being developed.
The fishing here – indeed pretty well
everywhere along the seaboard – is
excellent; the hikes along the cliffs faces
and over the rolling hills memorable.

And it is one of these hikes through
the hills that takes you to the village of
Coffee Bay, which gets its name from a

ship that was once wrecked on the coast, spilling its cargo of coffee beans. The village is popular with visitors for the excellent swimming, surfing, sailing and fishing spots along its beachfront. Here you'll find two small hotels and a number of beach cottages that are generally only in use during holiday season, at which time the place comes alive.

Hluleka Nature Reserve and Marine Sanctuary

This is one of the prettiest reserves found along the coast. Accommodation is either in self-contained, stilted wooden chalets with stunning views of the main beach and out over the ocean, or in small and very old rondavels (traditional-style round huts) set close to the shoreline. Newer and perhaps rather more unsightly huts have also been erected nearby. An old farmhouse serves as venue for the administration offices; viewed from its back veranda, the landscape drops away

down steep hills that look out over a small floodplain and magnificent coastal forests. This is one of the few places along the South African coastline where you can still hear the eerie, but at the same time raucous, sound made by the increasingly rare tree hyrax.

The beaches and beach activities are the highlights of Hluleka. Here you'll find some wonderful places to swim, fish and snorkel. However, there are also pleasant hikes over the hills, many of which will take you to small private coves where you can spend the day without seeing another soul.

ABOVE Like other watercourses along the Wild Coast, the Umgazi River, a few kilometres south of Port St Johns, crashes its way down the mountains only to end up in a languid estuary.

ADVENTURES WITH THE AMADIBA

One of the most beautiful, if not the most dramatic, stretches of the Wild Coast can be covered on horseback. The trail is run by the local Amadiba community, who hire out their own horses. One of the guides will collect you and your party at the mouth of the Mzamba River, near the Wild Coast Casino and Hotel (see p. 87), pack everything in saddlebags, and, after crossing the river, lead you on the 21-kilometre trail to Mtentu.

There's one overnight sleep-over, in tents at a stunning little camp near the coast at Kwanyana. Your food is provided, and cooked, for you. Also provided is a simple (rather rustic) hot shower and basic toilet facilities. Next morning you set off again, with a packed lunch, through landscapes of memorable beauty. Part of the trail leads along pristine, unspoiled beaches, part through the rolling hills and small Xhosa villages of the hinterland. You usually stop for lunch and a swim near the shipwreck at the Sikhombe River mouth.

The ride ends at the welcoming Mtentu River Camp, perched on the cliffs above the river. The views are superb. Again, you can paddle a canoe upstream to see the waterfalls or, if you wish, the guides will take you fishing. The local women look after you, very nicely, at both Kwanyana and Mtentu.

If you have a four-wheel drive (there is no access for ordinary saloon cars), you can bypass the horseback trail and book straight into Mtentu.

introduced from elsewhere, among them blesbok, blue wildebeest and Cape mountain zebra, which often graze on the short grass outside the chalets. Silaka's plant life – orchids, lilies, red-hot pokers, mosses, lichens – is enchanting. The rest-camp comprises 14 thatched bungalows, each with either a pleasant forest or an ocean view.

PORT ST JOHNS

You reach the Wild Coast's biggest town, which takes its name from a famous wreck (the *São João*, in 1552), from Umtata (see below) via the tarred R61. This is a very attractive settlement situated at the Umzimvubu River mouth, in a valley lush with subtropical plantings and patches of dense indigenous woodland. It has three good beaches, a nine-hole golf course, bowling greens, tennis courts, and roadside stalls that sell an enticing array of local rugs and basketware. Standards have perhaps dropped since its day as a premier tourist spot, but improvements are underway and it is well worth a visit.

TOP *A long and winding road leads up to this lookout spot above Port St Johns and the Umzimvubu River.*
ABOVE *The Umgazi River Bungalows: an ideal family holiday venue.*
BOTTOM *A Xhosa woman enjoys her traditional long-stemmed pipe.*

Umgazi River Bungalows

This well-known Wild Coast family resort – an extremely popular one, especially among honeymooners – is run by folk who really understand what a good beach holiday is all about. It's a small hotel, situated on the sprawling banks of the Umgazi River and surrounded by green lawns, tennis courts and a deck overlooking the river. The fishing is excellent.

The Mgazana mangroves are just along the beach; a morning's hike north will bring you to the Silaka Nature Reserve (see below). There is a ferry to take you across the river estuary, and canoes can be hired.

Silaka Nature Reserve

This small protected area lies just over the hill from Port St Johns Second Beach, from where the noted five-day trail to Coffee Bay once began. The hike is currently being restored, and in fact many people are already following it, even though most of the huts are still in a state of disrepair.

There are also shorter trails, some of them quite lovely, through the reserve itself, leading you past giant forest figs and over little moss-filled streams, and a rather strenuous walk up Heartbreak Hill and then down to the prominent landmark known as Sugarloaf Rock. Just a few kilometres further on is the wreck of the *Horizon* and the nearby Umgazi River Bungalows.

The reserve is home to quite a number and variety of wild animals, some

UMTATA
Nelson Mandela Museum

One of the few venues of sight-seeing note in Umtata, the capital of the one-time 'republic' of Transkei, is the restored Bhunga Building in Owen Street, which has been converted into a wonderful museum dedicated to struggle leader, statesman and international icon Nelson Mandela, whose home village, Qunu, is not too far away.

The museum is divided into three sections, the first housing the countless documents affirming the honours bestowed on the great man by universities and other organizations throughout the world; the second an exhibition displaying the myriad gifts Mandela has received from his admirers, among them heads of states, as well delightful artworks dedicated to him by children. The third wing is named The Long Walk to Freedom, which features enormous boards displaying extracts from Mandela's autobiographical work of the same name. Visitors can listen to the inspiring story, partially narrated by

Mandela himself. Some of the exhibits are illustrated with photographs taken during the struggle years (several of the photographers were placed under house arrest for this media coverage). There are also rare video-taped interviews with Mandela, and with other well-known liberation leaders.

MKAMBATI NATURE RESERVE AND MARINE SANCTUARY

Like other Wild Coast conservation areas, grasslands cover much of the 8 000-hectare Mkambati, but the reserve has one unusual feature – it is one of the very few places in the world where a waterfall, in this case Horseshoe Falls, crashes over the cliff face and straight down into the sea. Actually it isn't a single fall but a series of cascades and a scatter of crystal-clear pools that invite the bather and picnicker. Coastal forest clings to the sides of ravines, and there are unique patches of swamp forest in the lower-lying areas.

The reserve is bounded by the Msikaba River in the south and the Mtentu River in the north. The Pondo coconut *Jebaeopsis caffra* occurs naturally along these two rivers, and nowhere else in the world.

One can paddle a canoe up the Msikaba River for about two kilometres, until you get to a series of rapids. Watersports are of course popular along the river reaches; motorboats are permitted on the wide Mtentu River. Waterfalls, again, are a graceful feature.

Visitors have a number of accommodation options. There are thatched rondavels at the largish Riverside Camp, and stone cottages at the main camp. One old stone lodge, which overlooks the Msikaba River mouth, has its own swimming pool.

Wild Coast Casino and Hotel

This large, super-sophisticated hotel and leisure complex is set beside a limpid lagoon right on the seafront between the Mzamba and the Umtamvuna rivers, which separate the provinces of KwaZulu-Natal and the Eastern Cape. It has all the amenities and diversions associated with resorts of the grander kind, including a quite excellent, indeed championship,

golf course; tennis, bowls, squash, freshwater and ocean bathing, watersports, gaming rooms, restaurants, theatre, show-bars. Vehicles are not allowed on the beach owned by the hotel, nor, according to a new law, anywhere else.

The Mzamba River forms the southern border of the hotel grounds, and here you can (if you're lucky) pick up the most amazing fossils. A little further down the beach, on the flat, rocky shoreline, are the fossilised remains of a forest estimated to be 45 million years old – they are a declared national monument.

ABOVE *The wreck of the* Jacaranda, *just one of many ships that have come to grief along this treacherous stretch of coast.*

USEFUL CONTACTS

Jeffreys Bay
Tel: 042 293 2588
Fax: 042 293 2227
jbay-tourism@agnet.com
www.jeffreysbaytourism.com

St Francis Bay
Tel: 042 294 0076
Fax: 042 294 0675
stfrantr@intekom.co.za
www.stfrancistourism.com

Port Elizabeth Tourist Information Office
Tel: 041 585 8884
Fax: 041 585 2564
information@tourismpe.co.za
www.ibhayi.com

Bay World (oceanarium)
Tel: 041 586 1051
Fax: 041 586 2175
sandy@bayworld.co.za

Bay Charters
Cell: 082 574 1987

Shamwari Game Reserve
Tel: 042 203 1111
Fax: 042 235 1224
shamwaribooking@global.co.za
www.shamwari.com

Addo Elephant National Park
Tel: 042 233 0556
Lucium@parks-sa.co.za
www.parks-sa.co.za

Gorah Elephant Camp
Tel: 044 532 7818
Fax: 044 532 7878
res@hunterhotels.com
www.gorah.com

Tourism Grahamstown
Tel: 046 622 3241
Fax: 046 622 3266
info@grahamstown.co.za

East London Tourism
Tel: 043 722 6015
Fax: 043 743 5091
eltour@mweb.co.za

African Coastal Adventures
Tel/Fax: 043 748 4550
aca@africoast.co.za
www.africoast.co.za

Wild Coast Meander
Tel: 043 743 6181
Fax: 043 743 6188
meross@iafrica.com
www.wildcoastholidays.co.za

Wild Coast Toursim
Tel: 047 531 5290/2
Fax: 047 531 5291
ectbwc@icon.co.za
www.ectourism.co.za

Nelson Mandela Museum
Tel/Fax: 047 532 5110
mandelamuseum@intekom.co.za

Trennery's Hotel
Tel: 047 498 0004
Fax: 047 498 0011

Ocean View Hotel
Tel/Fax: 047 575 2005
oceanview@coffeebay.co.za
www.oceanview.co.za

Wavecrest Hotel
Tel/Fax: 047 498 0022
wavecrest@pixie.co.za

Morgan's Bay Hotel
Tel: 043 841 1062
Fax: 043 841 1130
MB.hotel@mweb.co.za
www.morganbay.co.za

The Haven Hotel
Tel: 047 576 0006/7
Fax: 047 576 0008
thehaven@wildcoast.com
www.morganbay.co.za

Umgazi River Bungalows
Tel: 047 564 1115/6/8
umgazi@iafrica.com
www.umngazi.co.za

Amadiba Adventures
Tel: 039 305 6455
Fax; 039 305 6456
rone@pondocrop.org.za

Bulolo Beach Holiday Camp
Tel: 047 564 1245
Fax: 047 5641314

The dining room at Assegai Lodge, near Grahamstown.

Southern Splendours

The Garden Route and Little Karoo

*T*he highway that runs from Cape Town east to Port
Elizabeth leads you through one of the world's most
attractive coastal strips, a visually stunning region of
bays and secluded coves, cliffs, golden sands, pastures and
dense forests and a necklace of inviting resort centres.
Inland there are the high mountains of the Langeberg,
the Outeniqua and the Tsitsikamma and, beyond, the
largely rainless but immensely fertile plains of the
Little Karoo basin, home to the ostrich farmer and the
wine grower. Farther to the north are the magnificent
heights of the Swartberg.

The Garden Route and Little Karoo

Mossel Bay, George, Knysna, Plettenberg Bay, Tsitsikamma,
Little Karoo, The Swartberg

The long coastal segment of the lovely route – the N2 national highway – begins at Mossel Bay and ends in the Humansdorp area some 250 kilometres to the east. Good roads lead inland, over grand passes through the mountains, to the Little (or 'Klein') Karoo and beyond to the towering Swartberg range.

MOSSEL BAY

This coastal hub has two claims to fame: it's been voted the country's second most popular holiday town, and, according to *The Guinness Book of Records*, it enjoys one of the mildest all-year climates in the world, second only to Hawaii. It is also steeped in history – originally home to an indigenous, semi-nomadic Khoi community who relished the local mussels (hence 'Mossel'), it served as a watering place for the Indies-bound European seafarers of the 16th century, later as a fishing village, and later still as a premier resort centre. The fairly recent discovery of offshore oil deposits has enhanced its industrial base, but it remains a major tourist drawcard.

The greater Mossel Bay area embraces some fine beaches – Santos, Pavilion, Die Bakke, Dias, Hartenbos, Kwa Nonqaba, and Reebok among them – which, apart from their sun-drenched charms, are good places from which to spot whales, dolphins and seals (best viewing site is probably The Point).

Cape St Blaize Cave

When Portuguese explorer Bartolomeu Dias landed on the southern coast in 1488, he found a group of pastoral Attaquas living around this striking cave, now a national monument, near Mossel Bay. Archaeologists, who have excavated it, believe it was originally used between 100 000 and 70 000 years ago, as a shelter, by hunter-gathering communities of Strandlopers, or Khoi-San people. The gaping hole, carved into the cliffs by the harsh elements, overlooks the waters of

DIVING WITH THE GREAT WHITES

The awesome great white shark is found along the entire coast of South Africa, and visitors to Mossel Bay can (depending on the season) view these sinister but perhaps much-maligned creatures up close. Shark Africa offers day-long cage-diving expeditions off the coast near Seal Island, about a kilometre from the shore. Because divers are enclosed in a floating steel cage, they do not need an Open Water certificate – simply a pair of goggles – to observe the predators in their underwater environment.

The cage – a steel 'fence' – is permanently attached to a platform on a 12-metre yacht, and is open at the top for easy exit (just in case you lose your nerve!). Great whites vary in length from about 2.5 to 6 metres, and although they do not 'attack' the cage, they are inquisitive and will approach within a metre or so. Wetsuits, dive gear and refreshments are included in the price of an excursion; onlookers – partners or family members – are welcome to come along on the trip.

the Indian Ocean. Boardwalks have been constructed and signs erected for visitors. The cave is easily accessible from the car park at The Point.

Bartolomeu Dias Museum

A visit to the museum complex, which comprises four different sections, is both an entertaining and an enriching experience. In the Shell Museum and Aquarium there is a wonderful display of seashells and the way they have been used by humans through the ages. The Culture Museum offers, among much else, a 'Crime and Disaster' walking trail around town, revealing the darker side of Mossel Bay's past (shipwrecks, a ghost lady, a brutal murder and so on) together with exhibits depicting the lifestyles of the early Khoi-San.

In the Maritime Museum you'll find a life-sized replica of Dias's caravel, a broad-beamed little sailing ship (guided tours by arrangement). The old granary houses exhibits that illuminate fynbos plant species endemic to the area and, eclectically, early wagon trails over the mountain passes. The town's maritime

traditions are honoured in the Model Shipyard Factory and its showroom, which is full of handcrafted, historic little vessels – the only exposition of its kind in the country and a fine place for children and adults alike (model kits on sale).

Other sites include the Malay Graves, which were discovered and excavated in 1968, and the weathered gravestones of the Lazaretto Cemetery (1809). Cape St Blaize Lighthouse, built in 1864, is a well-known landmark, as is the Post Office Tree, a massive milkwood under which passing sailors once left their letters for collection and delivery.

AROUND GEORGE

There are some exquisite drives and hikes through the countryside around George, the 'capital' of the Garden Route. Attractions in the town itself include the splendid collection of Ruby Reeves fairy paintings, in the local museum, that draw their inspiration from the glorious floral

OPPOSITE, TOP Mossel Bay draws industrial strength from its harbour, but the town and its flanking beaches remain a prime tourist venue.
OPPOSITE, BOTTOM The Cape St Blaize lighthouse and, below, its historic cave, first occupied more than 70 000 years ago by hunter-gatherer folk.
PREVIOUS PAGES The Keurbooms River mouth and the inviting sands of the Tsitsikamma area. In the background are the Tsitsikamma Mountains.

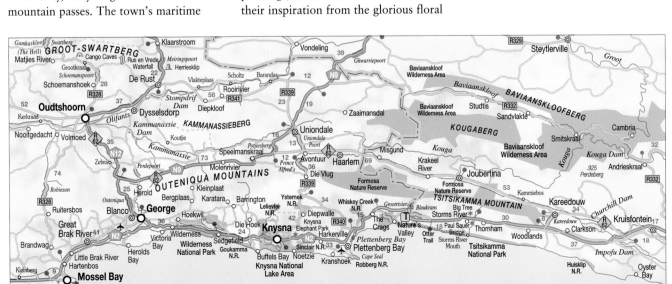

TOP These Fancourt guest suites overlook the 17th hole of the Montagu course. ABOVE The Links golf course at Fancourt – chosen venue of the 2002 President's Cup. BELOW Aerial view of the splendid lakes, mountains, forests and beaches of the Sedgefield area.

diversity of the of the surrounding hills and valleys. Also at the museum is a charming ethno-botanical garden display that shows how the early indigenous Kwena and San peoples used plants for medicinal and culinary purposes.

Scenic drives of special note include the trip over Montagu Pass (built between 1845 and 1847), which takes you through lush forests, over the mountains, and past such spectacular national monuments as the old Toll House and the Keur River Bridge. Also recommended is the drive along Seven Passes Road on the old Main Road between George and Knysna. It took the great road engineer

Thomas Bain 15 years to complete a masterpiece that winds through dense indigenous forest and beautiful ravines. It too is a national monument.

There are a number of superb hiking trails in the area, among them the Cradock Pass, George Peak Pass to Pass, and Garden Route Dam. All are graded, and all traverse the region's indigenous forests and its mountains.

Fancourt Hotel and Country Club

Situated at the foot of the Outeniqua Mountains near George, the Fancourt estate embraces one of the country's most prestigious golf and leisure resorts. It has four world-class golf courses (one of which, the Links, was selected to host the international 2002 President's Cup), five top-quality restaurants and any number of up-market leisure activities.

Fancourt offers the complete golfing experience: warm-up areas, putting and chipping greens, greenside and fairway bunkers and a full-length driving range. There's also a Golf School, with professional tuition, and an undercover driving range. If you're not a golfer, though, there's much else to enjoy – the health and beauty spa, heated Roman bath, Jacuzzi, sports such as tennis, volleyball, squash, billiards, swimming and so on. It's also a place for the family (supervision is provided for children). Two of its most spectacular features are the gardens and the scenic beauty of the wider surrounds. Golfing, and the restaurant, are open to non-residents.

KNYSNA AND SURROUNDS

Set on the banks of the Knysna estuary, gateway to the limpid and lovely Knysna Lagoon, heart of the Knysna National Lake Area and jewel of the Garden Route, the town was once an important (albeit dangerous) small harbour that served the timber trade. Ships would pass, at their peril, through the magnificent Heads, two massive sandstone cliffs that loom like sentinels over the estuary.

Today Knysna is a thriving centre of the tourist industry, its hub perhaps the Knysna Quays Waterfront development (which has replaced the old working harbour) and its shops, restaurants and fast-food outlets. It is from here that most of the charter boats sail; nearby is the station from which the Outeniqua Choo-Tjoe (see further on) departs on the journey to George.

Sedgefield

A pleasant seaside centre, west of Knysna, much favoured by the quieter kind of holidaymaker, Sedgefield is home to Cherie's Riding Centre, which caters for the family (including those who have never ridden before) and offers a choice of horse-riding routes: lake, mountain, forest, and beach. Close by is the very popular Swartvlei and its myriad holiday resorts; farther away lies Groenvlei, a popular bass-fishing freshwater lake, and, 12 kilometres on, the attractive sands of Buffels Bay. These stretches of water are part of the extensive and beautiful Wilderness Lakes Area.

Outeniqua Choo-Tjoe

A fun day-excursion out of Knysna is a journey on the Outeniqua Choo-Tjoe, a delightful, narrow-gauge, Class 24 steam train that follows the timber route that linked the town with George in days gone by. The trip takes two and a half hours (one way), and takes you through an enchanting forest and field countryside. Make sure you arrive at the station well before departure time (the seaside window seats are the best) as the train fills up fast. The excursion is reasonably priced; bar facilities and refreshments are available on board.

Knysna Seafood

Knysna is renowned for the delicious oysters harvested, since 1949, by the Knysna Oyster Company from its lagoon and estuary, its fame celebrated at the annual Oyster Festival in January. Visitors may embark on a fascinating conducted tour of both the oyster beds, and of the factory where these seafood delicacies are cultivated and processed.

Featherbed Nature Reserve

A pleasant boat trip across the Knysna Lake to the western section of the Heads will bring you to the privately owned Featherbed Nature Reserve. In fact, the reserve is really only accessible by ferry, the entire excursion lasting about four hours and taking in a 4x4 drive up the steep slopes – with the most spectacular views of Knysna, the mountains, the lake and the sea – and the return trip. From the top of the Head, there is an easy,

TOP Knysna's estuary and lake system: a nature-lover's paradise.
ABOVE The vintage, narrow-gauge Outeniqua Choo-Tjoe on its way to George.
BELOW The Heads, two sandstone cliffs, dominate the mouth of Knysna's lagoon.

ABOVE Abseiling down cliff faces in the Featherbed Nature Reserve, with the sea crashing against the rocks below, is an adrenaline-pumping experience.
TOP RIGHT So, too, is the bunjee jump off the Bloukrans River Bridge, at 216 metres, the highest in the world.
BELOW The Knysna Elephant Park offers a unique safari, on which one can walk with the elephants as they feed and move through the sanctuary.

optional, 2.2-kilometre guided nature walk through indigenous forest, onto the cliffs, past the caves and along the rugged coastline. Look out for the Knysna lourie, a colourful forest bird, and the blue duiker, South Africa's smallest antelope. For the less energetic, the four-wheel-drive vehicle will do a full round trip. Both the walk and the drive end up at the reserve's restaurant (orders are taken on the ferry).

Other excursions run by Featherbed include a 'historic' cruise, on the lagoon and out to the Heads, which evokes something of the days when Knysna was a busy little port.

Abseiling and Cruising

The more intrepid kind of visitor may abseil a heart-stopping 122 metres down the cliff face in the Featherbed reserve, which is where S.E.A.L. Adventures runs its challenging operation. The views alone – if you dare to look down – are worth the effort. You can either canoe in with S.E.A.L or meet them at the site. Preparation includes a full safety brief and a couple of test runs off smaller cliff faces (the 30-metre abseil from Beachcomber Caves and the 55-metre one from Needlepoint). As an optional extra, guides will also take you on a morning quad-bike ride through the spacious forest plantations and the mountains around Knysna.

Rather less energetic are the many opportunities for boating and sailing. On offer, among much else, are trips on the lagoon or out to sea in Springtide Charters' 50-foot *Outeniqua*, a luxury yacht with three double cabins and a large saloon. Choices include a day-sailing or overnight excursion, sunset cruise, and a champagne breakfast. All trips depart from the Knysna Quays.

Knysna Elephant Park

The last of the true Knysna elephants, once prolific in the area's dense forests, recently died, and today the only real opportunity you will have to see the animals – or rather, their replacements – in what was once their natural environment is in the Knysna Elephant Park. The sanctuary is 22 kilometres from town, off the N2 that leads to Plettenberg Bay. At present there are three adults – Harry, Sally and Duma – and a 'small' but very fast-growing calf called Satara.

There are no barriers separating visitors from these magnificent creatures, all of them relocated from the Kruger National Park. An attractive viewing option is the rather exclusive sunset or sunrise (two- to three-hour) Elephant Safari, a walking trail that leads through the surrounding forests and valleys.

PLETTENBERG BAY

'Plett', as it is fondly known, is a beach-lover's paradise. Fairly wind-free, it has long stretches of soft sand – perfect for

sunset strolls – which give way gently to azure seas that host catamarans and body-surfers, boogie-boarders and, further out, whales and dolphins. Disc-shaped, pure white pansy shells, found only in a very few places along the southern Cape coast, dot the sandy shores. Be warned that in summertime Plett's beaches are packed.

More than 37 species of whales and dolphins have been recorded off the coast of Plettenberg Bay. Bottlenose and humpback dolphins can be seen all year round, and schools of common dolphins visit the bay regularly. Bryde's and minke whales, too, visit the bay in all seasons, while the southern right whales arrive each year, between June and November, to calve and breed.

Humpbacks bypass the coast during their annual migration, and it is these animals that usually impress with their spectacular performances, breaching, lobtailing and flapping the water with their fins.

Because the Robberg Peninsula shelters the bay, it is possible to view these marine mammals – in fairly calm waters – by boat, often approaching really close to a group of playful dolphins or a pod of gentle sea-giants (though one has to observe a number of sensible protective restrictions). Several boat-based whale- and dolphin-watching operators work out of Plett, including Ocean Safaris in association with the MTN Centre for Dolphin Studies (researchers sometimes come along). Otherwise, you can always find an independent a skipper and

knowledgeable guide. The tours, which accommodate a maximum of 12 people, leave from the beach; lifejackets and liquid refreshments are provided.

Robberg Nature Reserve offers walking trails, pretty beaches, caves used by the early indigenous inhabitants, and, on the sandstone promontory, a colony of Cape fur seals.

Nyati Distillery

This rustic distillery, set on the Buffalo Hills Game Farm near Plett, turns out a unique range of 'mampoer', a powerful type of schnapps that was originally made from endemic fruit but is now

ABOVE Flying with the seagulls on thermals and up-draughts in the Ocean Blue motorised glider over the Plettenberg Bay area – a sublime way of sightseeing.
BELOW LEFT It is possible to get close to whales, dolphins and seals by boat, several of which launch from Plettenberg Bay's main beach.
BELOW The Robberg Peninsula, a nature reserve, offers walking trails through indigenous flora, lookout points for viewing whales and dolphins, and a resident seal colony.

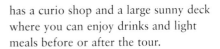

based on a much wider range of fruits (notably on peaches). It's a fun place to visit if you're open to a few carefree hours: the famous (or infamous) Jack's Jungle Juice, or 'JJJ', is produced in various flavours and can be tasted. You may also eat some good traditional food and sample Nyati's 'mampoer' and 'witblits' ('white lightning') in the restaurant. Book in advance.

Monkeyland

Just 16 kilometres outside Plett is the first primate sanctuary of its kind in the world, a place where monkeys roam free within their natural environment. Electric fencing ensures that the animals don't escape, and you can walk through the forest, stopping at water holes, hides and raised viewing platforms to watch the delightful inmates leaping around in the trees, playing, feeding and resting in the branches. The sanctuary is home to many species from several continents; some individuals have been bred in captivity before being 'released' at Monkeyland.

One sometimes has to search for them, but the search is well rewarded when, for instance, an odd-looking Madagascan black lemur (also known as an indri), or a small South American squirrel monkey emerges from cover.

The 'rangers' who lead the tour groups explain all about the residents, their origins, social behaviour and habits. They also tell some tragic stories of captive monkeys and their difficulty in adapting to the semi-wild. Monkeyland

has a curio shop and a large sunny deck where you can enjoy drinks and light meals before or after the tour.

Plett from the Air

A sightseeing flight over the Plettenberg Bay area in a motorised glider is an experience to be savoured. The craft is so small you almost feel you yourself have wings – an impression reinforced by the low, just-above-beach-level flight. In season, one can swoop over the schools of cavorting dolphins and the many small pods of whales that come into the bay. At other times, and especially at sunset, the deep-green, mysterious indigenous coastal forests beckon the airborne visitor.

There are two glider operators in Plettenberg Bay, one operating from the airport and the other from Stanley Island.

Another fine way to explore Plett from the air is in a light aircraft – either a Piper Tri Pacer (4-seater), or a Piper Aztec (6-seater). In fact, this is perhaps an even better option than the glider because you can go further and see more. A flip around the area will also take you over the bay to see dolphins and whales, and over the Robberg Peninsula and the forests, but instead of turning back near Nature's Valley, as the glider does, you'll soar above the high Gourits River gorge and watch the adrenaline-filled bunjee-jumpers at play (see further on).

There are daily Ramble Africa shuttle-flights to Tsitsikamma, mainly for those joining the Storms River Adventures tours, and an excursion flight to Oudtshoorn to see the Cango Caves and other local sites. It is, however, quite possible to arrange a route of your own because the tour company can take you to almost any place you want. An especially enjoyable excursion is that from Plettenberg Bay airport to Shamwari Game Reserve (see page 81), or Gorah (page 82) in the Addo Elephant National Park near Port Elizabeth.

Keurbooms River

This makes its way to the sea through the soaring gorges of the beautiful Keurbooms River Nature Reserve just north of Plettenberg Bay. Its banks are lined with giant yellowwood trees and with secluded little white beaches and rocky outcrops. A wealth of indigenous

plants clamber up the steep cliffs. You may explore and enjoy this river on your own, aboard a hired canoe or small motorboat with a packed picnic lunch, or by ferry with a guide who will explain something about the prolific plant and bird life of the area. The latter is a 10-kilometre trip and takes about two and a half hours. The reserve has a camp site.

TSITSIKAMMA

The Tsitsikamma National Park, which runs for about 75 kilometres along the coast between Nature's Valley and the Groot River, embraces rivers and streams that cut through deep ravines, cliffs with caves gouged into them and a coastline that is a haven for an enormously rich and colourful variety of marine life. Its magnificent natural beauty inspires outdoor leisure activities, among them fishing, snorkelling, hiking, kayaking, and black-water tubing.

One can get from Plett to Nature's Valley along either of two routes; one follows the main toll road (N2), the other, older one is a beautiful winding road that weaves down through the Groot River Pass, which is graced by splendid indigenous forests (the trees include handsome yellowwoods),

waterfalls and little bridges that span dark, almost treacle-coloured watercourses. One may fish in a small area alongside the Storms River Rest Camp; a snorkelling trail and a diving route have been charted along the coast. Keen hikers can follow the famed Otter Trail (see below), the Loerie Trail, and the Tsitsikamma Hiking Trail.

The Otter Trail

One of the country's oldest, most popular and rewarding hikes, the five-day Otter follows a 42-kilometre route from Storms River Mouth to Nature's Valley, along the rugged and spectacular coastline between the Tsitsikamma park's seaboard, making its way over rivers, hills, cliffs, beautiful beaches, rocky ridges, deep pools. The vistas are magnificent, and, here and there, one can spot the elusive Cape clawless otter.

The longest day's stretch is just 14 kilometres, but the route can be quite strenuous in parts. One overnights in comfortable rustic huts, but you have to carry everything you need (there are no facilities). And, since it's not a round trip, you need to arrange your own return transport from Nature's Valley. Book well in advance; the waiting list is usually about a year.

TOP Waterfalls and natural forests grace the Tsitsikamma park.
ABOVE Black-water tubing on the Garden Route's Storms River.
BELOW The shy and elusive Cape clawless otter, for which the Otter Trail is named.
OPPOSITE, TOP Nature's Valley, with its beautiful vistas of sea and fynbos, is at the end of the famed Otter Trail.
OPPOSITE, CENTRE This ringtailed lemur is one of many different primates to find sanctuary at Monkeyland.
OPPOSITE, BOTTOM The Keurbooms River cuts its way through the lushly beautiful Langkloofberge.

ABOVE The Little Karoo – still very much ostrich country.
BELOW Children outside their home in the little settlement of Schoemanshoek, near the Cango Caves.
BELOW RIGHT A guided tour around the Cango Wildlife Ranch; the crocodile enclosure is a favourite with visitors.

Adventure Sports

The rivers along the Garden Route are a deep, clear brown colour, much like the that of mollasses, apparently the product of organic plant materials that leech into the water. The phenomenon gives its quality to an increasingly popular sport – blackwater tubing (as opposed to white-water activities such as river rafting).

A tubing excursion with Storms River Adventures begins with a steep descent into the almost inaccessible canyon cut by the Storms River. 'Tubers' are issued with safety helmets and wetsuits (sometimes two each in cold weather) before embarking on their exhilarating trip down the canyon, the adventure ending at the suspension bridge in the Tsitsikamma National Park.

Storms River Adventures also organise diving and boat trips, mountain-bike rides over the rugged countryside, abseiling excursions down deep gorges, marine tours and a 'woodcutter's walk' through the forests.

Then there's bunjee-jumping – the ultimate thrill in adrenaline sports – and if a 94-year-old woman can do it, anyone can. The Bloukrans River Bridge, just 40 kilometres north of Plettenberg Bay, is the focus; the jump, at 216 metres, is the highest in the world. The minimum

weight for a jumper is 40 kilograms, the minimum age 14; expert guidance and supervision are at hand.

But if leaping into the void is a bit too daunting, there are other adventurous ways to enjoy the river and its surrounds from the bridge. Some folk prefer to be attached to a high-tensile steel cable and lowered into the gorge; others to stroll with a guide along the walkway at the top of the arch; both afford spectacular eagle-eye views over the magical forests far below.

INLAND TO THE LITTLE KAROO

The ostrich-feather boom of the late-Victorian and Edwardian eras put Oudtshoorn, 'capital' of the Little Karoo – and a most pleasant place overlooked by the beautiful Outeniqua Mountains in

the south and the mighty Swartberg in the north – very much on the map. Since the decline (though by no means the disappearance) of the industry, the Cango Caves have taken over as the area's major drawcard, enticing some 250 000 visitors each year to Oudtshoorn. However, the town is almost as well known as host to the annual and sparkling Klein Karoo National Arts Festival.

Ostrich Farms

There are about 400 such farms in the Oudtshoorn area, nurturing some 90 000 of the big birds, although not all the properties are accessible to the public. Most of those that are – the show farms – run tours. There is usually a visit to a breeding camp, where a male and female, and their massive eggs, are kept in isolation. At the Safari Ostrich Farm you can watch a chick hatching out (behind glass). The trip usually ends with a visit to the fields to observe the birds in their natural habitat, followed by a demonstration and a perhaps a jockey ride (which, fun though it is, seems a bit tough on the creature).

Feather Palaces

In its heyday the feather industry made an instant millionaire of many an Oudtshoorn resident. Especially rich were the ostrich-farmer barons and feather merchants, many of whom spent their money on what today are referred to as 'feather palaces', hugely opulent and elaborately decorated, but not always tasteful, mansions of turrets, towers, teak panelling and stained-glass windows. Few have survived the years, but you can still see a little of this extravagant past in and around town.

The Cango Caves

The complex, a vast network of interleading passages and massive caverns, was formed more than 650 million years ago, when this part of the continent was still submerged beneath the sea. Time and water have sculpted the porous limestone into an incredible fairyland of columns, crystal curtains and a fantasia of flowstone formations. There is some controversy over who actually 'discovered' the labyrinth, but what is known is that the large entrance cave was

used as shelter by early Khoi-San people. Standard tours are led by knowledgeable and often amusing guides, each hour on the hour in season. The caves are a bit hot and humid, so wear sensible footwear and light clothing.

Advance booking is recommended. On site there's plenty of parking, a family restaurant, coffee shop, bar, curio shop, crèche and kennels. The museum and interpretative centre offer useful background information on both this and other cave formations around the world.

Cango Wildlife Ranch

Don't be put off by the massive, rather kitsch crocodile-head that marks the entrance to the ranch. Inside it is all

ABOVE Over the millennia, the action of water has carved a fantasy world at the Cango Caves.
BELOW Feeding time at Oudtshoorn's Safari Ostrich Farm.
BOTTOM A few 'feather palaces' can still be seen in and around Oudtshoorn.

tasteful enough; the enclosures are clean; the animals well cared for. Most of the guides are locals, many are multilingual, and all of them are interesting, knowledgeable and friendly.

A tour begins at the crocodile pools and moves on to the snakes and other reptiles (among them a giant albino python and a bizarre prehensile-tailed skink) and then to the big-cat enclosures. The ranch is said to be one of the world's top five cheetah breeding centres, and even if you don't really enjoy seeing these magnificent animals in captivity, it's still quite a thrill to get close enough to pat them (under supervision). In residence are other endangered animals, such as the pygmy hippo, African wild dog, serval and aardwolf.

Klein Karoo Wine Route

The route, one of the country's eight such, is just as impressive though of course rather less well known than the wineways nearer Cape Town. It stretches along the R62 from Montagu to De Rust near Meiringspoort, and some fabulous port, wine and 'witblits' farms welcome you. 'Witblits', or 'white lightning', is so-named because of its high alcohol content (50 per cent proof). It strikes hard.

Moreover, many of the farms are not as commercialised as the bigger Cape cellars. Grundheim, which has been in the Grundling family for five generations, is one such, producing excellent and well-priced brandies, muscadel and port, its recipes for home-made liqueurs and 'witblits' earning numerous national prizes. A tour of the farm, in the company of a family member, is a truly South African experience not to be missed. It usually ends with some wine tasting buttressed by home-made biltong (sun-dried meat), cheese and hilarious stories.

THE SWARTBERG AREA

The Swartberg Pass was built, as were many of the elevated roads through the mountains of the Cape, by the famous Thomas Bain. The pass, one of several grandly scenic routes in the region, was opened in 1888, and offers some of the most spectacular views over the Little Karoo to the south.

Kobus se Gat Veld

This restaurant provides a most delightful, and unusual, stopover on the road between Oudtshoorn and the Swartberg Pass, and owner Kobus is one of the area's most fascinating characters. His rustic pad, perched a little way up the pass with memorable vistas over valley and mountain, offers traditional country hospitality and delicious 'traditional' food – cooked over an open fire (there is no electricity). The menu includes *roosterbrood* (bread baked over hot coals), Karoo lamb, ostrich kebabs, steaks, game sausages and a feast of salads. The restaurant is very much a family venue; book in advance.

Gamkaskloof (Die Hel)

Gamkaskloof is the Swartberg's 'ghost town'. The first farmer settled in this area in 1830, and the last left in 1991. In its heyday, its fertile soils supported about 120 people, a small school, and a water mill. The 'Gamkasklowers' were an almost entirely self-sufficient community. They farmed and traded wheat, rye, fruit and vegetables, seeds, dried beans and peas, nuts and honey. There was no road access to the outside world; all produce was carried in and out of the valley either on foot or aboard donkey caravans along two routes, one of which ran along the river, which often came down in flood, the other through a gorge with a very steep footpath known as Die Leer.

In 1962 a proper road was finally constructed, but instead of encouraging development, it prompted a gradual exodus. When the last farmer vacated this lovely hidden valley, Cape Nature Conservation began buying up properties in an effort to rescue and maintain the rich cultural fabric of the area.

Today, visitors may stay in one of the valley's quaint, charmingly restored cottages or at the camp site. The dirt road leading to Gamkaskloof is long and rather arduous, but well worth the effort if it's a reasonably priced, perfectly quiet getaway you're looking for. Annetjie Joubert, the only genuine Gamkasklower still in residence, has turned the original family homestead into pleasant self-catering accommodation. She provides a traditional Gamkaskloof breakfast.

Prince Albert

The attractive village of Prince Albert can be reached either via the Swartberg Pass or the wonderfully scenic Meiringspoort, a pass that runs through

the steep orange-and-gold sandstone gorges of the mountains.

Many of the town's Cape Dutch, Karoo and Victorian buildings have either been beautifully preserved or restored, and 19 of them are national monuments. The immediate area produces fine crops of olives, peaches (January), grapes (March), figs, apricots. The locals are deservedly proud of their sun-ripened fresh and dried fruit, their homemade cheeses and their Karoo lamb. Among visitor options are star-gazing, fossil-hunting, mountain-biking and hiking. An interesting excursion is the tractor ride to one of the surrounding farms – the trails start from De Bergkant Lodges and Cottages, a beautifully restored homestead at the village entrance. The tours are organised on an ad hoc basis.

ABOVE The road into the Gamkaskloof, or 'Die Hel', is steep, long and arduous.
OPPOSITE, TOP The scenic splendour of the Swartberg range.
OPPOSITE, CENTRE Grundheim Farm, on the Klein Karoo Wine Route, makes excellent wines and liqueurs, including a powerful 'witblits' ('white lightning').
OPPOSITE, BELOW The pleasant reaches of the Gamka River, with the Swartberg in the distance.

USEFUL CONTACTS

Note: regional tourism offices will supply contact details for the many and various destinations covered in this chapter.

Garden Route and Klein (Little) Karoo Regional Tourism
Tel: 044 873 6355/14
Fax: 044 884 0688
info@gardenroute.org.za
www.capegardenroute.org

Shark Africa (shark diving)
Cell: 082 455 2438
sharkafrica@mweb.co.za

Klein Karoo Wine Route
Tel/fax: 028 572 1284
info@kleinkaroowines.co.za
www.kleinkaroowines.co.za

Whale Hotline
Cell: 083 910 1028

Forest and Mountain Tours
Tel: 044 535 9631
fmtours@cyberpark.co.za
www.cyberpark.co.za/fmtours

Kleinplaas (accommodation)
Tel: 044 272 5811
Kleinplaas@mweb.co.za

Chalets in Tsitsikamma National Park.

The Gentle Land

The Overberg

*T*he name 'Overberg', in the language of the early
Dutch settlers, means roughly 'the other side of the
mountain'. It refers to the then little known but always
gentle, and bountiful, countryside of lofty coastal rampart,
hill, dale, forest plantation, green pasture, orchard,
vineyard and scenically lovely seashore that lies to the
east of the high Hottentots-Holland range. The main
centres are the coastal town of Hermanus, ranked among
the world's most rewarding whale-watching venues and,
inland, the gracious old settlement of Swellendam.
Bisecting the region is the N2 national highway.

The Overberg

Hermanus, Grootbos, Cape Agulhas,
Arniston, De Hoop Nature Reserve, Still Bay

The N2 freeway linking Cape Town and Port Elizabeth takes in the entire southern coastal plain, its route running in part through the fynbos veld that makes up much of the famed Cape Floral Kingdom, in part beneath high, blue-hued mountains, and in part along an Atlantic coastline, whose bays and beaches charm the senses with their beauty.

ABOVE Huge southern right whales come close inshore to mate and calve in winter and spring.
BELOW Walker Bay's cliffs provide fine vantage points for whale-watching.
BOTTOM RIGHT Hermanus is one of South Africa's premier holiday towns.
PREVIOUS PAGES Yellow canola blooms beautify the Overberg's fertile valleys.

HERMANUS

Hermanus is one of the Cape's most popular holiday destinations, and as mentioned probably the best whale-watching destination along the country's entire coastline. It plays host, in particular, to the giant southern rights – so called because they are rich in oil and slow-moving, and the early whalers considered them the 'right' whale to hunt – which come close inshore during the winter months both to mate and to calve.

Especially good land-based vantage points are the high cliffs above the town. But if you'd like a closer acquaintance with these great, gentle and oddly graceful marine mammals, try one of the boat trips that a local enterprise lays on. Excursions set out three times a day (depending on the weather) from the new harbour, taking passengers over the blue waters of Walker Bay, and to within metres of the animals themselves.

Walker Bay, actually, is more than a whale-watcher's paradise. It is also home to the fearsome great white shark, and a number of operators offer boat-based cage-diving forays, affording the more intrepid sightseer close-up views of this protected species.

It is eminently worthwhile strolling around the village itself. In season, you will probably see and hear what is believed to be the world's only official 'whale crier', a herald with placard and kelp-horn (and cellphone) who tells all within earshot of the arrival and location of the southern rights, 20 or more of which can sometimes be observed at one and the same time.

Also of interest is the Old Harbour. Hermanus was once the lively centre of the fishing industry – the offshore Algulhas Bank is one of the richest fishing grounds on earth – but was fairly recently supplanted by a stylish new marine

THE BROAD ACRES OF GROOTBOS

Grootbos, named after the reserve's indigenous white milkwoods (they form the world's largest forest of the species), lies less than two hours' drive from Cape Town and about 13 kilometres from the little town of Stanford.

The reserve, extending over rather more than 1 000 hectares of unspoilt natural environment, is home to the country's largest private fynbos garden, a magical place graced by ponds, medicinal herbs, a nursery, and the milkwood forest, some of whose trees are hundreds of years old.

This family-owned reserve can host just 28 guests, so personalised attention is pretty well guaranteed. If you can bear to tear yourself away from the beautiful rooms – built of locally hewn timber and stone – there is plenty to see and do: boat trips out to Dyer Island, whale-, dolphin-, and great white shark-watching, horseback riding, hiking and swimming in the reserve's charming little pool.

BELOW The seal colony at Dyer Island is no doubt one of the drawcards for the great white sharks (bottom) that are so plentiful in the area.

complex. The Old Harbour, though, is still there, maintained as a kind of open-air museum full of veteran working boats lovingly restored to their original, sturdy condition, and haven to an endearing collection of resident Cape fur seals.

A variety of outdoor sports is on offer at and around the new harbour. Elsewhere, venues of special interest include the tasting rooms along the smallish and newish Hermanus Wine Route that winds its way through the scenic Hemel-en-Aarde Valley. Hermanus is also the venue for the annual and hugely popular Whale Festival, a celebration that involves music and markets, crafts, sports and flower exhibitions. It is usually held over a dozen or so days in September.

CAPE AGULHAS

Cape 'Agulhas', which means 'needles' in Portuguese (presumably reflecting the early seafarers' fear of the sharp reefs that bedevil the offshore waters), is the African continent's southernmost tip, and the official longitudinal point at which the Indian and Atlantic oceans meet. There isn't in fact a great deal to see here – the coastal plain just slips quietly into the ocean to become the great, shallow Agulhas Bank. But the marvellous old (1848) limestone lighthouse, part of the Bredasdorp museum complex (it's the only lighthouse museum in Africa), is

worth a tour for its artefacts. The surrounding countryside is now protected within Agulhas Plain National Park, at present still a loose conglomerate of lands covering the plain itself and much of the coastline.

The park remains undeveloped; there are no camp sites or National Park accommodation facilities. However, there are still a good number of places to stay within the park – in villages such as Struisbaai, L'Agulhas and the nearby Arniston (or Waenhuiskrans).

The Agulhas Plain has a rich diversity of plants – some 2 000 different kinds altogether, including more than 110 Red Data Book species. The wetlands that dot the plain are home to the endangered Cape platanna, to the micro-frog, and to a number of rare coastal birds such as the striking-looking African black oystercatcher.

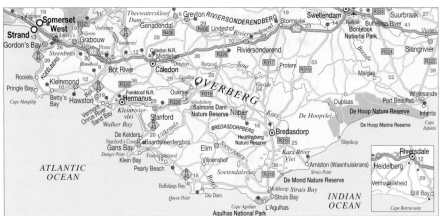

TOP This view towards Arniston is typical of the region's seascapes.
ABOVE Waenhuiskrans, a cave large enough to house an ox wagon.
BELOW Time has stood still in the delightful little settlement of Elim.

ARNISTON

Arniston is a trendy holiday destination where many Capetonians own smart beach houses overlooking the little fishing harbour and pretty swimming beaches. Just along the sands is a massive cave from which Arniston took its original (and a still alternative) name – Waenhuiskrans ('Wagon-house Cliff'). The early settlers maintained that the cave was big enough to accommodate an ox-wagon. It is a short walk, from the main beach car-park, along the sands to the cave. The local hotel has a fine reputation, and deservedly so.

The older part of the village, known as Kassiesbaai, overlooks the harbour and the wide bay from its vantage point on the cliffs. This is where many of the local fisherfolk live – in the thatched and white-washed cottages built by their ancestors. Tours are conducted around Kassies Baai (the whole village is a national monument) during which one can meet and chat to the locals, and visit the old, weather-worn, sea-salt battered stone church. The cliff-top is also a fine place for whale-watching.

To get a real feel of the community, make your way down to the harbour either early in the morning to see the boats set out, or in the evening when they bring in the catch.

You can buy fish straight off the boats for an instant barbecue.

DE HOOP NATURE RESERVE

The entire 40-kilometre stretch of the De Hoop Nature Reserve and its offshore waters is a protected area. The reserve, famed for its myriad endemic fynbos plants, is also home to many mammal species. Moreover, the Atlantic waters here host an extraordinary number of southern right whales from May through to October.

A number of hiking and mountain-biking trails run through the reserve. There's also a recently opened 'whale trail'. Other routes include the Vlei Trail, which, although it has shorter variations, is 15 kilometres in its entirety and takes hikers past the 16-kilometre-long vlei, a stretch of marshy terrain partly situated in a gorge flanked by high limestone cliffs. Today the vlei lacks an outlet to the sea, and is thus a unique ecological system in the Cape context. The wetland is recognised by the Ramsar Convention as an area of international importance.

The Coastal Trail winds along the beach past the vast sand dunes at Koppie Alleen, and there are ample opportunities for hikers to swim and snorkel in the rock pools (swimming off the beach is considered unsafe).

Finally, there's the Potberg Trail, which leads up to the top of the Potberg peak (600 metres above sea level) from where there are stunning views of the Breede River. The Potberg sustains 12 endemic plant species, together with the southwestern Cape's only breeding colony – 24 pairs – of Cape vulture. The wider reserve also supports black eagle, black-shouldered kite, and jackal buzzard.

Accommodation in De Hoop comprises camp sites, self-catering cottages, and a lodge – Lekkerwater – situated right on the beach.

THE EELS OF STILL BAY

The exquisite Still Bay, situated some 200 kilometres from Swellendam (you get there via Riversdale and the R305), may be off the beaten track but it is well worth a visit.

Whales are a feature of marine life here, of course – as they are all along the southern coast – but they're not the only water creatures for which the area is renowned. One intriguing oddity is the eels that populate some of the streams running through and near the village. Many of these so-called 'sea-snakes' are incredibly 'tame' – some can even be hand-fed! The best place to see them is in the stream in front of the historic Palinggat Residence, one of Still Bay's two national monuments and a good example of Strandveld architecture, which is quite unique to the region.

Also special are the ancient fish traps built by the original Strandloper ('Beach Walker') inhabitants. The *vywers*, as the traps are known, are dams built of stones to form a simple barricade between high- and low-water marks. As the tide recedes, fish are caught in the artificial pools.

During the season Still Bay is full of holidaymakers enjoying the excellent

beaches and making good use of the splendid fishing venues. There are tours into the adjacent fishing village of Melkhoudtsfontein, most of whose residents are descendants of the original Khoi inhabitants.

Melkhoudtsfontein locals have established a small botanical garden, Soete Inval, that contains indigenous plants used for generations for medicinal and culinary purposes. The best time to visit the garden is between June and October, when the plants are flowering. The small graveyard in the village is also fascinating – many of the fishermen's graves are decorated with sea shells. A quaint craft shop sells a lovely range of handicrafts and home-baked products.

TOP A walk through De Hoop's dunes and fynbos will delight anyone with an interest in Cape flora and fauna.
ABOVE While rare, the blue crane, South Africa's national bird, is often seen in the Overberg region.

USEFUL CONTACTS

Peninsula Tourism
Tel: 021 788 6193
Fax: 021 788 6208
peninsulatourism@yebo.co.za

South African National Parks
The Agulhus National Park
Tel: 012 343 1991
Fax: 012 343 0905
reservations@parks-sa.co.za
www.parks-sa.co.za

Hermanus Tourism Bureau
Tel: 028 312 2629
Fax: 028 313 0305
infoburo@hermanus.co.za
www.hermanus.co.za

Grootbos Private Nature Reserve
Tel: 028 384 0381
Fax: 028 384 0552
grootbos@hermanus.co.za
www.grootbos.com

Whale Hotline
Tel: 083 910 1028
info@cape-whaleroute.co.za
www.cape-whaleroute.co.za

Whale Boat Trips
Contact Hermanus Tourism

White Shark Cage Diving
White Shark Ecoventures
Cell: 082 658 0185

**White Shark
Diving Adventures**
Tel: 028 384 1005
Fax: 028 384 0614
jpb@iafrica.com
www.dive.co.za

Cape Agulhus Lighthouse
Tel: 028 341 0705

Arniston Tourism Bureau
Tel: 028 445 9999
Fax: 028 445 9797

Kassiesbaai De Hoop
Tel: 028 542 1126/7
Fax: 028 542 1247
dehoopinfo@sdm.dorea.co.za

Still Bay Tourism
Tel: 028 754 2602
Fax: 028 754 2549
infosb@telkomsa.net

Elim Tourism Bureau
Tel: 028 482 1806

The Mother City

Cape Town and Surrounds

*C*ape Town, the country's oldest and arguably most
attractive city, nestles elegantly beneath the majestic
and often moody heights of Table Mountain, the flat-
topped massif that served as an unmistakable landmark
and symbol of refuge for generations of seafarers. Today,
the metropolis ranks as one of the southern hemisphere's
premier tourist destinations, known for the beauty of
its surrounds, its historic buildings, its lively waterfront
and harbour, its theatres, restaurants and nightspots,
and for the inviting wine routes of a hinterland
that has its own myriad charms.

Cape Town and Surrounds

Table Mountain, Cultural Cape Town, V&A Waterfront, Robben Island, Kirstenbosch Gardens, Constantia, Atlantic Seaboard, South Peninsula

The city sprawls around Table Bay at the tip of Africa and at the northern end of a narrow, 60-kilometre-long peninsula whose shores are, according to popular belief, lapped by two oceans. The region is endowed with an excellent road network; the N1 highway – heir to Cecil Rhodes's celebrated Cape-to-Cairo route – connects it with Johannesburg and points north, and its air links are well developed.

ABOVE The cableway is the most popular way of ascending Table Mountain.
BELOW The view from Signal Hill at sunset, as the city's lights come on, will linger in the memory.
PREVIOUS PAGES The rugged terrain of the Table Mountain range.

TABLE MOUNTAIN

The mountain, flanked by two sentinel-like heights known as Devil's Peak and Lion's Head, rises more than 1 000 metres above city and bay, and its distinctive, often cloud-wreathed summit measures over three kilometres from end to end. The vistas that unfold from the top are unparalleled.

There are a number of ways of reaching the summit. Some 300 hiking and walking trails of varying degrees of difficulty wind their way up the steep slopes at the back (or southern side). Most of the routes are easy enough, but some are hazardous, demanding real climbing expertise; others should be challenged only with the help of an experienced guide. Most people, though, make the ascent via the cableway, which was inaugurated way back in 1929 and recently upgraded. The Table Mountain Aerial Cableway Company now operates two 65-seater cablecars with rotating floors that allow passengers a panoramic view over the city during the four-minute ride. You cannot pre-book, so if the weather looks fine, head for the mountain early. In peak season, queues are quite long, but the most you'll have to wait is about an hour. Pack a windbreaker – whatever the weather below, it can be cool on the summit.

At the top there's a self-service restaurant and a well-stocked (but perhaps expensive) gift shop from where you can send a fax or write a letter that bears the Table Mountain postmark. Again, the vistas are splendid, taking in the city and harbour below, Robben Island to the north, the regimented, massive features known as the Twelve Apostles to the south and, in the distance, the cliffs of Cape Point. To the east is the wide sweep of False Bay and, beyond, the smoky, blue-grey hills of the Hottentots-Holland range. The slopes are also a showcase for the Cape Floral Kingdom,

the smallest but most diverse of the world's six botanical regions.

Table Mountain alone sustains 1 470 different species of the unique fynbos ('fine bush') vegetation, to which the endemic sugarbird and orange-breasted sunbird are drawn. Here, too, are a number of small mammals, including the dassie or rock hyrax (the animal is highly adapted to the steep sandstone heights), the genet and the occasional and elusive caracal (a medium-sized and very agile cat).

CULTURAL CAPE TOWN

The city offers a huge amount in the way of theatre, art, and music; its galleries and museums are among the country's most inviting. Call in at Cape Town Tourism's Visitor Centre in Burg Street for all the details. Here, the focus is on just three destinations.

Bo-Kaap

Situated on the southern slopes of Signal Hill and overlooking central Cape Town is one of the oldest of the city's suburbs – Bo-Kaap.

Informally (though incorrectly) known as the Malay Quarter, its narrow alleyways and charming little flat-roofed houses began making their appearance when newly freed slaves of the Dutch East India Company moved into the area more than two centuries ago. It is now home to a section of the Cape's large Islamic community.

The Bo-Kaap Museum is housed in the suburb's oldest building (1760). Don't wander around the area on your own; it is more enriching (and safer) to hire a guide, who may well introduce you into the homes of residents, and escort you to community gatherings that would otherwise be inaccessible in this close-knit community.

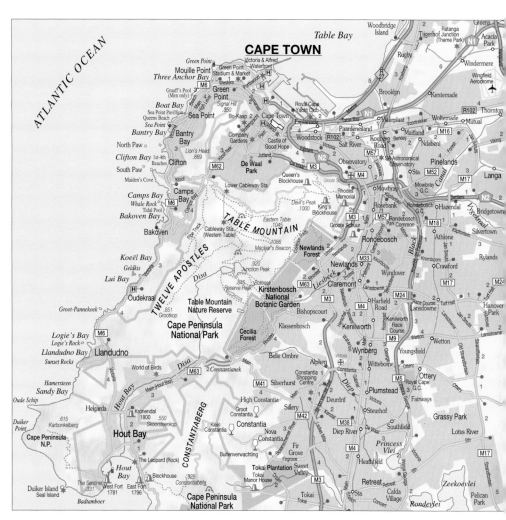

ABOVE Most of Bo-Kaap's flat-roofed homes date back to the 18th century.
TOP LEFT Many gracious old colonial buildings can be seen in Cape Town's city centre, especially along Long Street.
LEFT Greenmarket Square, in the city centre, bustles with street traders. Pictured is a traditional hair-stylist at work.

ABOVE *The Victoria & Alfred Waterfront is part of a working harbour, busy with craft of all shapes and sizes. Table Mountain looms in the background.*

District Six Museum

For those interested in South Africa's recent past, a visit to the museum is a good place to start. On display are reminders that, not too long ago, a vibrant, mainly working-class community lived, worked and played on the city's eastern fringe before the bulldozers of the apartheid regime moved in to destroy their homes. District Six was declared a 'white' area; its people – there were some 60 000 of them – were forcibly relocated over the years to the sandy, windswept, largely desolate Cape Flats.

Many ex-District Six residents and their descendants are intimately involved with this 'living museum', which serves as a venue for gatherings of various sorts.

Exhibits are regularly updated as new artefacts and mementoes are unearthed and donated.

Township Music Tours

Unlike Durban and Johannesburg, Cape Town's African 'townships' do not have many established venues of historical interest. However, what the city does offer the visitor is a tour to its musical heart.

Which is not to say that there's nothing else to see in the historically 'black areas'. On the contrary, a number of tour operators take groups around the standard community projects and the amenities, and to sample the fare at a restaurant or shebeen (tavern) in Langa, the oldest residential development, or Khayaletsha, the newest. However, a fascinating and remarkably fresh way to experience township life is to join a musical excursion.

The initiative of the New World Music Foundation, a typical tour includes a visit to a 'drum circle', where a master drummer will run an interactive 'workshop' that gives an insight into indigenous African instruments and the sounds they produce.

From here the visit moves to a private home or to one of the township's restaurants for a home-cooked African meal, and ends at a tavern, where visitors and their hosts dance and party to the rhythm of some of Africa's most exhilarating music. If you haven't the

THE DAY OF THE MINSTRELS

One of the most exuberant of Cape Town's celebrations is the annual Coon, or Minstrel, Carnival. On the second day of the New Year thousands of people get together in bands, or troupes, to parade, sing and dance around the streets. Green Point Stadium is their eventual destination, and their costumes are the ultimate in colourful extravagance.

For months beforehand, the groups have practised their *moppies* – vaudeville-style numbers sung mostly in Afrikaans and accompanied by banjos, drums and whistles. The music, the routines and the dress are rooted in the joys and tribulations of the Cape's distinctive 'coloured' community, but they also draw something from the minstrel traditions of the American Deep South. The carnival is a visible reminder of a way of life that finally disappeared, along with District Six, in the 1960s.

time or don't want to do the whole trip, you can arrange to visit one of the clubs or jazz dens and mingle with the musos.

V&A WATERFRONT

One of the oldest parts of Table Bay harbour has in fairly recent times been transformed into a vibrant, cosmopolitan, largely traffic-free and entirely tourist-friendly complex of malls. Here you'll find craft and produce markets, museums and marinas, umbrella-shaded quayside bistros, restaurants, pubs, fast-food eateries and nightspots, theatres, cinemas (including the giant-screen Imax), entertainment centres and some of the country's most stylish hotels, all set against the magical backdrop of Table Mountain.

Steam trains (occasionally) depart from a point near the Victoria & Alfred Waterfront on their vintage runs; helicopters take off and land with their sightseeing passengers; charter, cruise and fishing boats, salt-stained tugs and squeaky-clean leisure craft line the docksides or bustle backwards and forwards in what is still a working harbour. Smallest and best-known of the boats is probably the Penny Ferry, whose successive oarsmen have been rowing folk across Victoria Basin for generations.

Start at the information centre near the Telkom Exploratorium, where you get a good idea of the Waterfront's geography and what it has to offer.

Two Oceans Aquarium

A walk through Two Oceans has an element of dreamlike fantasy about it. Kelp (seaweed) billows in huge acrylic tanks, predatory sharks weave their way through schools of fish, enormous Japanese spider crabs skitter by on their spindly legs, seals splash and preen in and around the rock pools, and thick, slumberous eels lurk in dark caves.

The place is organised in nine major galleries, which between them sustain more than 3 000 living specimens representative of a myriad species of fish, invertebrates, mammals, birds and plants that live in the waters off the Cape coast. Among the displays is a giant living kelp forest, and the 'Story of Water' featuring the recreation of an ecosystem that links mountain streams and intertidal zones with the sea, and which is inhabited by penguins, African black oystercatchers, catfish and the relevant plant life. The 'touch pool' allows youngsters to hold a starfish or a sea urchin in their hands, and to feel the texture of different types of seaweed.

The predator tank is always popular, particularly at feeding time (daily at three in the afternoon). Ragged-tooth and other sharks catch the eye, but there are also shoals of yellowtail, garrick, turtles, several species of ray and much else in residence. Visitors can walk through the semi-tunnel that surrounds the tank for close-up views through the massive, curved acrylic panels, from the sides and

ABOVE Dragon-boat racing at the Marina in the Waterfront.
ABOVE LEFT Visitors relax in front of the kelp tank at the Waterfront's Two Oceans Aquarium; soft music complements the gentle swaying of the seaweed growths.
BELOW Victoria Wharf, the Waterfront's premier mall, is open till late.
BOTTOM A launch tour is just one of many ways of exploring the bright and busy Waterfront complex.

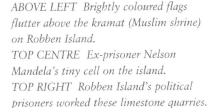

ABOVE LEFT Brightly coloured flags flutter above the kramat (Muslim shrine) on Robben Island.
TOP CENTRE Ex-prisoner Nelson Mandela's tiny cell on the island.
TOP RIGHT Robben Island's political prisoners worked these limestone quarries.

underneath. On the downward ramp you'll see strange, deep-water fish, and a model of the mysterious coelacanth.

An alternative – albeit fairly expensive – way of getting to know the sharks is to dive in with them, under supervision. You'll need a diver/scuba certificate (aquarium staff can help arrange a day-long resort course if necessary). Three divers are taken in at a time. Advanced divers may also help official volunteers to feed fish in the giant kelp forest. Wetsuits, tanks and other gear can be

hired, or you can use your own. A bit more complicated, and even more pricey, is the 20-minute Copper Helmet Dive for Open Water 1 divers (you go down in a genuine Imperial Navy Diving suit – copper helmet, lead boots, canvas suit and umbilical air cable). Book at least two days in advance.

One can also take a behind-the-scenes tour to see how the millions of tons of fresh seawater is cycled through the tanks, and how the fish are kept healthy and well fed.

FUN AND FANTASY AT RATANGA

South Africa's first full-scale theme park, Ratanga Junction, is located in the vast Century City complex in Cape Town's northern suburbs. It's a real family venue, packed with fun and fantasy attractions, kiddies' rides, snake and bird shows, restaurants, fast-food outlets and quirky shops, all of which appeal to both the young and the young at heart. Rides range from gentle bumper-car drives to the adrenaline-pumping Cobra, a suspended, looping coaster that catapults its passengers, feet flying free, from a height of 34 metres along 910 metres of track at four times the force of gravity and breathtaking speeds of close to 100 kilometres an hour.

You're not allowed to bring food or drinks with you, and it is suggested you enter with little more than your wallet (there is nowhere to leave your bag when you're on a ride). Backpacks and bags can be stored in prepaid lockers at the entrance. Some of the best rides involve water and lots of splashing, so it's a good idea to take some waterproof gear along as well, although plastic covers can be bought inside the theme park. Refreshments are readily available, as mentioned, but they tend to be a bit on the pricy side. The entrance fee is variable, according to the season, but it usually includes the rides.

The entrance fee to the Two Oceans is on a par with that of a cinema ticket. There's a restaurant just off the foyer.

ROBBEN ISLAND

South Africa's most illustrious political prisoner – charismatic statesman, democrat and international icon Nelson Mandela – brought Robben Island into the global spotlight, but in fact the two-kilometre-wide, four-kilometre-long island has a recorded history going back more than 400 years. Apart from serving as a political prison, it has over time done duty as a leper colony, a mental institution and a military base. Today it is a nature sanctuary, World Heritage Site and a memorial to South Africa's liberation struggle.

The island can only be explored with an official, organised tour group. Tours leave from the Waterfront. The ferry takes about 25 minutes, the tour around the island a further two-plus hours, and is divided into two sections. The first part takes in the historic island village, and includes a visit to the infamous lime quarry in which the prisoners were forced to work, the male leper church, the

lighthouse, and various World War II fortifications and relics. The bus then stops at the island's rocky shoreline, where visitors can enjoy (on a clear day) a superb view of Cape Town's seafront suburbs, Table Bay Harbour, Table Mountain, Signal Hill, Lion's Head, and the Twelve Apostles.

From here visitors go on to the prison section, probably the most interesting part of the tour. During the apartheid years, Robben Island's prison held both criminal and political inmates; you are led through by guides who themselves were once incarcerated here as political prisoners. Hearing at first-hand their real-life experiences adds an extra and fascinating dimension to the visit.

A-section of the notorious maximum-security area comprises 40 isolation cells that contain artefacts on loan from ex-political prisoners, re-creating the bleakness of prison life. B-section includes the tiny cell in which Nelson Mandela spent 18 of his 27 prison years. There is a photographic display featuring many other leading contemporary political figures who were once both interned and, even more soul-destroying, isolated from their fellow inmates.

TOP Table Mountain viewed from Robben Island. The island is rich in history, and in bird life, serving as home to one of the few land-based colonies of the endangered African penguin.
ABOVE Robben Island's lighthouse blinks out its warning to seafarers. Even so, many ships have come to grief off the perilously rocky coastline.

*TOP Some of the walks at Kirstenbosch
Gardens are an easy stroll; others cross
Skeleton Gorge on their way to the summit
of Table Mountain.*
*ABOVE The bright orange strelitzia is one
of many thousands of flower and tree
species to be seen at Kirstenbosch.*

KIRSTENBOSCH GARDENS

Kirstenbosch National Botanical Garden,
situated on the eastern slopes of Table
Mountain in the Newlands-Constantia
area, is a 528-hectare estate established in
1913 to conserve and promote the
indigenous flora of southern Africa – and
it has become world famous for doing so.
It embraces about a third of the country's
18 000 plant species, including those of
the famed fynbos group (among them
the multi-specied proteas and ericas).

The relatively small cultivated section
is devoted to plants of the different
vegetation regions, many of them rare
or endangered species. Other plants and,
especially, many fine trees grow 'wild' on
the upper slopes.

The developed grounds are well
organised in theme areas – the Protea
Gardens, the Cycad Ampitheatre (holding
a splendid collection of these most
ancient of plants), the rock garden, the
herb garden and so forth. For the visually
impaired there is a Fragrance Garden and
a Braille Trail. Strollers have an
embarrassment of riches from which to
choose; among the myriad routes are the

Fynbos Walk, a stroll to a delightful
little brick-lined natural spring called
(incorrectly) Lady Anne Barnard's Bath,
forest trails, and a couple of gravelled
routes, one of which leads through
Skeleton Gorge to the top of Table
Mountain. Conducted group tours
are laid on. The pathways are clearly
marked, but you can also hire a portable
acoustic aid called 'My Guide', which
tells you all about the various numbered
points on your route.

One of the many highlights of the
gardens is the glassed Conservatory,
especially designed to house succulent
plant species – including the strange
kokerboom, or quiver tree – that would
not otherwise survive in the Cape's
Mediterranean climate. The Conservatory
is also divided into regions, and includes
plants from high-altitude areas, shady
forests and the arid parts of southern
Africa. At the centre of the Conservatory
is one of Africa's best-known succulent
trees, the giant baobab.

At and around the fairly new and
rather impressive Visitors' Centre there
is a restaurants, a well-stocked shop, a

nursery, areas where flower shows and exhibits of botanical art are held, and a 'waterwise' demonstration garden. There is another restaurant situated inside the gardens.

Kirstenbosch hosts classical music and jazz concerts on late summer Sunday afternoons. Most visitors pack a picnic basket and enjoy the last of the sunshine on the garden's beautiful lawns before the performance begins. Arrive early, as the concerts are extremely popular.

CONSTANTIA

Groot Constantia is the senior of three grand old Cape Dutch homesteads which, together with a historic farm, comprise the Peninsula's wine route. The house itself, and its vineyards, date back to the 1680s, when it served as home to the able and imaginative Cape governor Simon van der Stel, whose kindly ghost (according to several 'eye-witnesses') haunts the long, oak-lined avenue that graces the grounds. The estate has always produced fine wines; features of your visit will include the main mansion (a period museum), the

architecturally notable two-storeyed cellar (a wine museum), pleasant wine-tasting, a meal in one of the two restaurants (the sophisticated Jonkershuis and the less formal Tavern) or a picnic beneath the shade trees.

The cellar is especially notable: it was designed by the talented French architect, Louis Thibault; the pediment, adorned by lively cherubs, was the work of the almost equally celebrated sculptor and woodcarver, Anton Anreith.

In summer, Groot Constantia also hosts jazz concerts and an especially worthwhile craft market.

The two other manor houses, smaller but in their distinctive way just as charming, are Klein Constantia, built in 1796 and fairly recently, and beautifully restored (tours by appointment), and Buitenverwachting, also splendidly restored and incorporating an award-winning restaurant.

Also on the route, and second oldest of the destinations (1688), is Steenberg farm, at the corner of Tokai and Steenberg roads. The farm is famed for the quality of its wines.

ABOVE The gardens at Kirstenbosch are arranged according to floral theme; pathways are clearly marked; guided tours are laid on.
BELOW Workers harvest grapes on the Groot Constantia wine estate, one of the country's oldest and most attractive.

ABOVE Clifton Beach, famous for its bikini-clad beauties. Sun-worshippers crowd the sands at the height of the summer season.

BELOW Bakoven (pictured below) is a secluded enclave adjoining the long stretch of beautiful, white Camp's Bay beach.

ATLANTIC SEABOARD

The Cape metropolitan beaches are renowned both for their golden sands and the beauty of their backdrop. The Atlantic (western) waters tend to be cooler than those of the eastern shores.

The inner Atlantic suburbs, Green Point and Sea Point, offer small, rocky stretches, but there is a graceful, palm-fringed promenade much favoured by Capetonian strollers.

A little way further south is pretty Bantry Bay and, next door, up-market Clifton, one of the few beaches (actually four secluded beaches, divided by rocks) on the Peninsula where the wind hardly ever blows. Yachts often anchor offshore. Clifton's Fourth Beach tends to be the most popular, but you'll have to walk down some fairly steep steps to get there. During peak season, it can be difficult to find parking close by, both at Clifton and at neighbouring Camp's Bay, one of Cape Town's most popular stretches – a wide beach, sheltered on each side by massive white boulders. There are a number of open-air cafés and restaurants along the palm-lined seafront road.

Victoria Drive

The road south hugs a scenically enchanting coastline. There are no houses; just one building (a rather smart hotel); on your right is the chilly, often turbulent Atlantic Ocean, its rollers crashing against the rocks and cliffs of the shoreline; on your left the land rises and then soars in a series of massive features known as the Twelve Apostles (there are in fact 17 of them), whose summits are

often wreathed in swirling clouds. About 10 kilometres along Victoria Drive is Llandudno, a charming and affluent seaside residential area occupying the steep slopes that run down to beach and bay. Again, there are attractive boulder features, good surfing, a shipwreck just to the south and, still further along (by footpath; there's no road access), Sandy Bay, popular among those who like baring all.

Hout Bay

The road over the hill and down into the wooded valley (it's still Victoria Drive) brings you to Hout Bay, a largish, pleasantly embowered town set beneath the high Constantiaberg.

Hout Bay harbour is very much a working area, home to a fleet of sturdy, honourably battered fishing boats but also to some handsome leisure craft. Above looms the distinctively shaped Sentinel peak; the dockside is rather commercialised but not offensively so – the Mariner's Wharf complex offers a fresh fish market (known for its crayfish, or rock lobster), an informal eatery and a fine restaurant. The quayside invites an

exploratory wander, especially at the magical sunset hour.

So too does the World of Birds, inland along Valley Road. The sanctuary, which ranks among the southern hemisphere's largest and most attractive bird parks, offers spacious walk-through aviaries that, between them, house more than 3 000 birds belonging to 450-plus species, many of them both exotic and colourful. Other creatures – primates and various small

ABOVE Llandudno, which is fairly difficult to access, is quieter than most beaches around the Peninsula, but no less beautiful. BELOW Hout Bay, seen in the distance, nestles beneath Constantiaberg, its fishing harbour a prime tourist destination.

TOP *Simon's Town's new harbour development offers shops and restaurants with splendid views across False Bay.*
ABOVE *Boulders Beach provides sheltered swimming among a tumble of rocks. Here, encounters with the endangered African penguin are virtually assured.*
TOP, RIGHT *The historic lighthouse at Cape Point.*

mammals, some of them convalescents from injury or deprivation – are also in residence.

THE SOUTH PENINSULA

The drive to Cape Point takes you through Newlands and other southern suburbs, over the memorably scenic Ou Kaapse Weg (Old Cape Road: the M64) and past the fringes of Noordhoek, which has the longest beach on the Peninsula. Then on to Kommetjie – a fishing village renowned for its crayfish (rock lobster) – and Scarborough, where the outlying Misty Cliffs is a favoured surfing venue.

The recommended return trip is along the M4, following the gentle False Bay coastline through the historic naval centre of Simon's Town, and then progressively through Fish Hoek, the quaint village of Kalk Bay (where the main street is lined with charming antique-cum-junk shops), quiet St James, with its wind-free beach, and Muizenberg, one of the Cape's most popular surfing and swimming venues. Muizenberg's white sands stretch on northwards, uninterrupted for a full 15 kilometres.

Silvermine Nature Reserve

Ou Kaapse Weg runs through the Silvermine reserve, a 2 000-hectare expanse that has been cleared of all alien vegetation (a signal victory for conservation) and is now in pristine condition, though the great fires at the turn of the millennium had their impact on the precious fynbos vegetation (pioneer plants are still in evidence;

BOULDERS AND THE AFRICAN PENGUIN

The sheltered cove at Boulders Beach, on the southern False Bay coast, has become world famous for its thriving colony of African penguins.

Once known as the jackass penguin (it makes a braying sound, rather like that of a donkey), the African penguin is listed in the Red Data Book as a vulnerable species, and the protected colony, which consisted of just two breeding pairs only 20 years ago, today numbers more than 3 000.

The beach is within walking distance of the coastal centre of Simon's Town. The birds, which are quite used to the human presence and nonchalantly mingle with visitors, sun themselves on the dazzling white sands and on the boulders for which the beach is named. They nest in the surrounding scrub-covered dunes, and swim off into the blue ocean to feed.

Possibly the best place from which to view the African penguins is from the Foxy Beach side of the Boulders area. Access to the beach is limited, and a small entrance fee is payable.

'normal' growth will take over completely in due course).

Silvermine is part of the wider, recently proclaimed Cape Peninsula National Park which embraces all the higher and wilder parts of the region – including the Table Mountain range and the Kirstenbosch gardens. The reserve spans the uplands (notably the Steenberg) that run across the Peninsula's narrow 'waist', and is hugely popular among weekend hikers and ramblers. A favourite walk is that to the heights above the reservoir, from where there are stunning views. The land (in normal times, and in the appropriate season) is graced by a quite splendid array of ericas and proteas, restios and springtime flowering bulbs; rather special are the pagoda trees, the golden conebushes and the winter-blooming blackbeard sugarbush.

On its southern stretch, Ou Kaapse Weg descends into the broad – and increasingly suburban – Fish Hoek Valley, where there are a number of quaint restaurants and shops (Longbeach Mall is the grandest development).

Cape of Good Hope Nature Reserve

The most spectacular feature within the reserve, though just one among many places of interest, is Cape Point, an enormous massif that looms over the blue waters off the second southernmost extremity of Africa (the southernmost is Cape Agulhas, to the east). At the base of the rise that takes you to the Point itself, and just off the main parking area, is the Two Oceans Restaurant and gift shop. Set into the mountainside, the restaurant offers sweeping views of False Bay, and, if you are there in season (May to October), you can spot southern right whales sporting in the ocean. Alongside the shop is a modern Visitors' Centre, from where you can send e-mail messages.

In the past, the only way to get up to the Point was by walking (strenuously), or in a shuttle bus known as the 'Flying Dutchman' – a reference to the legendary phantom sailing ship of that name, reportedly seen by some quite respectable people, including King George V. Today, however, a sophisticated funicular conveys passengers to the viewing deck. The steep climb from the deck up the steps to the historic old lighthouse is well worth the effort.

When driving through the reserve, keep a look-out for the chacma baboons. The Cape Peninsula's troops are the only protected population of these animals in Africa: they have unique foraging characteristics (they are largely dependent on marine foods) and a high tourism profile, but they can be over-familiar with visitors. While it is fun to watch them from the safety of your car, do not encourage them in any way or attempt to feed or get close to them. No matter how tame they seem, they remain wild, and potentially dangerous, animals.

A small fee is payable at the entrance.

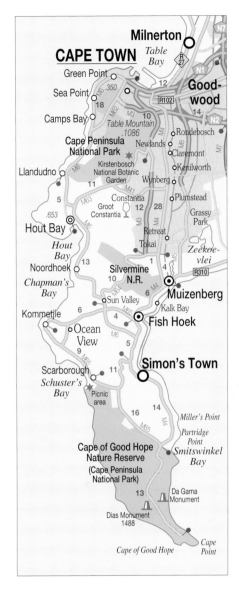

Land of the Vine

The Cape Winelands and Wineways

*A*n hour's drive to the east of Cape Town takes you
to some of the most sublime expanses of countryside
you are likely to see anywhere, a land of high mountains
and green valleys, and of vineyards and scented orchards
that, in autumn, are heavy with mellow fruitfulness. Here
too are historic towns and villages, and spacious, graceful
homesteads that represent the very best of the Cape Dutch
architectural idiom. The region is informally known as the
Winelands – and aptly so, for the products of the vines
are as notable as the scenic beauty.

The Cape Winelands and Wineways

Stellenbosch, Somerset West, Franschhoek, Paarl,
Breede River Valley, Major Wine Routes

Probably the best way to see and enjoy this magical part of South Africa is by following one or other of the wine routes. The main highway north is the N1; excellent roads connect the various urban centres and, in the great majority of cases, the individual farmsteads as well.

ABOVE The enchanting countryside between Stellenbosch and Franschhoek. BELOW The interior of Oom Samie se Winkel, one of Stellenbosch's oldest and most inviting shops.
PREVIOUS PAGES A patchwork of vineyards stretches away across the Stellenbosch countryside as far as the eye can see.

STELLENBOSCH

This is South Africa's second oldest town – founded in 1679 and named in honour of Simon van der Stel, the early Cape governor – and although the first white settlers grew wheat, they soon turned to the making of wine and, today, vineyards cover the surrounding hillsides

The town itself has matured gracefully over the centuries, its broad streets shaded by tall oaks and lined by buildings designed and constructed to resist the ravages of time. Many can be seen and enjoyed along Dorp Street and Die Braak, the old village green; among the more notable are four historic houses, now period showcases, collected together within the ambit of the Village Museum. Their gardens, charmingly, feature the trees, shrubs and flowers that adorned the original homes.

Rather more interactive are the Oude Meester Brandy Museum on the Old Strand Road, and an atmospheric little store called Oom Samie se Winkel ('Uncle Sammy's Shop') in Dorp Street, which sells a marvellous variety of items ranging from traditional home preserves to curios. The usually lively pub next door (De Akker) is also worth a visit.

SOMERSET WEST

This pleasant seaside residential centre, part of the Cape Town metropole, lies in the general Stellenbosch area and is a good starting-point for exploring the attractive resort village of Gordon's Bay, just down the coast, and the Hottentots-Holland range that towers over the area (the mountain road, for all its dizzy bends, is worth following for its quite splendid vistas). Recommended venues close to Somerset West include Helderberg Nature Reserve, scenically spectacular and home to an unusually rich plant life (some of the proteas are unique to the area) and a fine array of fynbos birds, among them the redcrested fluff-tail (three subspecies) and the protea seed-eater.

Close by is Vergelegen, a grand Cape Dutch manor house and estate that started life, controversially (it cost Governor Willem Adriaan van der Stel, or rather, the public purse, a fortune) in the early 1700s.

The grounds are exquisite; highlights are its Octagonal Garden, the herb garden, the Lady Phillips Tea Garden, the winery (very modern, even futuristic), and the venerable and lovely trees – camphors that were planted in 1700, oaks (of which one is the country's oldest specimen), the rare dawn redwood, and an ancient, twisted mulberry, sole survivor of a long-defunct silk-making enterprise.

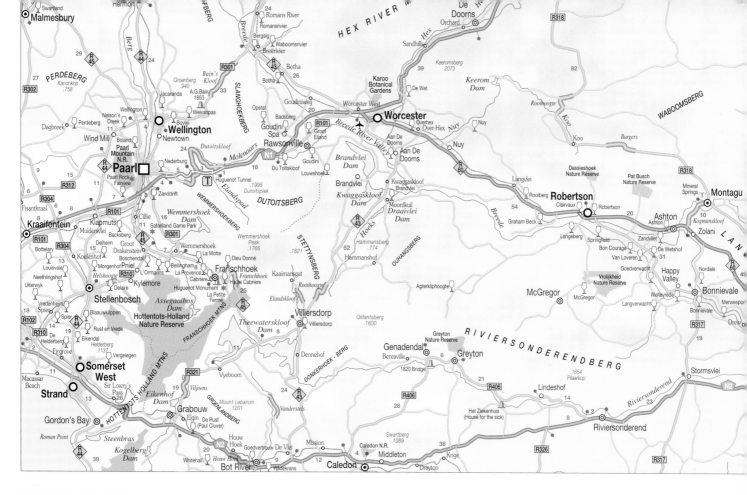

FRANSCHHOEK

Three centuries ago a small group of French Huguenots, who had escaped religious persecution in Europe, settled in a valley flanked by the beautiful Drakenstein Mountains not far from Cape Town, bringing with them their wine-making (and other) skills. From these humble beginnings came a tradition of viticulture that has helped elevate South Africa to the foremost ranks of the world's wine-producing countries.

The newcomers called their settlement Franschhoek ('French Corner'). Prime sightseeing destination in the charming little town is the elegant Huguenot Memorial and its museum complex. However, the immediate area is equally if not more renowned for its culinary traditions – an array of enchanting little auberges (guesthouses) and restaurants, most specialising in French and classic Cape cuisine, draw gourmets from afar.

PAARL

The largest of the Wineland towns – its jacaranda- and oak-lined main street is a full 10 kilometres long – also has a splendid monument, this one celebrating the powerful and ultimately successful movement that entrenched the Afrikaans language, or Taal.

Paarl takes its name from the massive, rounded, pearl-like boulders that surmount the mountain flanking the western part of the town. One drives to the summit through the Paarlberg Nature Reserve, known for the wealth of its fynbos plants and for the delightful Mill Water Wild Flower Garden. Among other notable venues are the Laborie manor house in Taillefert Street (headquarters of the giant KWV wine cooperative), La Bonheur Crocodile Farm, and the Bhabhathane Community Project, which offers a nice line in woven goods.

Bain's Kloof Pass

Just to the north of Paarl is the attractive town of Wellington, a hub of the dried-fruit industry and, for the hiker and motorist, the start of a scenically enthralling trip over Bain's Kloof Pass. The R303 high road runs northeastwards for 30 spectacular kilometres, descending into the dramatic hill-rock-and-ravine countryside of the Breede River Valley (see page 126). You'll find a pleasant picnic spot at the summit. Among the best of the area's hikes is the circular route through the Wolwenkloof.

BELOW Franschhoek's vineyards are illuminated by the late afternoon sunshine. BOTTOM A Cape vineyard heavy with the harvest.

125

MAJOR WINE ROUTES

The best-known (but by no means only) wine areas centre on the historic towns of Stellenbosch (almost 30 cellars), Franschhoek (16) and Paarl (20), and visitors are welcomed by the estates and farms, and invited to sample and buy their excellent wine on the spot. Most offer wine-tastings and tours; many have splendid restaurants; each has its own character, its own distinctive attractions. There are also numerous smaller, privately owned vineyards with outstanding wines on offer. Mentioned here are just a few of the vast number of destinations that are well worth visiting.

The Stellenbosch Route

One of the area's most visitor-friendly venues is Spier, a beautifully developed, picturesque estate that has gained international acclaim. Much more than just a wine farm, the Spier complex embraces a fine manor house, wine cellars, a wine and farm shop, restaurants, a magnificent rose garden, a cheetah park and equestrian facilities. The estate even has its own railway station. An excellent way to see the countryside is to board the steam train that leaves from the city's Monument station (behind Cape Town's Civic Centre in Old Marine Drive). The train chugs through the pretty countryside and you can spend the day tasting wine, enjoy a concert in the magnificent Spier Amphitheatre, and you won't have to worry about the night-time drive home!

Another old farm with an amphitheatre is the Oude Libertas complex, on the southern fringes of Stellenbosch, headquarters of a massive co-operative and home to the Cape Wine Academy. The concerts are mainly of classical music; the surrounding, lush green lawns an excellent location for summer picnics.

The Blaauwklippen estate, farther out, was established in the late 17th century and can be explored in a horse-drawn carriage that wends its way through the vineyard. Blaauwklippen also has a small but interesting coach museum. Simonsig, another prominent estate and one of the largest privately owned wine farms in South Africa, is almost as famous for its cheeses as it is for its wine.

ABOVE Theuniskraal's vineyards produce some of the Cape's more respected wines.
BELOW The Cape Flemish-style manor house at Boschendal. Both the estate's wines and its traditional buffet lunches are renowned.
BOTTOM Nederburg, host to the country's premier wine auction.

THE BREEDE RIVER VALLEY

The Western Cape's premier river nurtures an immensely fertile valley famed for its grapes and other fruits, and whose beauty – and that of its tributaries, notably the Hex River – matches its lushness. Near the headwaters in the high Ceres basin is the attractive town of Ceres, girded by mountains whose upper slopes are often snow-covered in winter, and which overlook great orchards of apple, pear, peach, cherry and other trees in the valleys below.

A short distance to the west is the upland town of Tulbagh, which hit the headlines in 1969 when an earthquake shattered many of its old buildings (the place was founded in the early 1700s). Those destroyed were rebuilt, the remainder carefully restored to match the originals, and today Tulbagh is blessed with a splendid array of proclaimed historic monuments, 30 of them along Church Street alone.

The third and largest of the valley's centres is Worcester, on the edge of the Little Karoo just off the N1 highway (and thus an inviting stopover for travellers to and from the northern interior). Notable among the town's visitor attractions is Hugo Naudé House (where many of this fine South African artist's works are on show) and the large and lively Kleinplasie open-air 'living' museum, a showplace of old-style settler (mainly Afrikaner) farming and domestic routines. Don't by-pass the Karoo National Botanic Garden just north of town – its succulent displays are world famous.

The Franschhoek Route

Among well-known estates along the route are Bellingham, an old but fairly recently rejuvenated estate that markets a fine range of labels, and Boschendal. After visiting Boschendal's Cape Flemish-style homestead, and touring the cellars (by appointment), you can enjoy a picnic basket in the charming, oak-shaded grounds – or a buffet luncheon that is famed for its lavish selection of traditional Cape dishes.

The Paarl Route

Paarl's Nederburg, a 200-year-old homestead nestled among the Klein Drakenstein Mountains, probably has the highest international profile of all South African estates – its wines have won many awards, and it hosts (in autumn) an annual wine auction, which draws buyers and visitors from all over the world.

Fairview, which occupies part of Paarl Mountain, provides a low-key introduction to wine-making – and it is one of the few places where children will feel comfortable, partly because it has an entertaining 'goat tower', a spiral structure up and down which the animals clamber. There are goat-milking sessions in the afternoons, and Fairview produces a superb line of goat cheeses.

ABOVE Van Loveren, on the Robertson Wine Route near the pleasant town of that name in the Breede River Valley.

USEFUL CONTACTS

Winelands Regional Tourism
Tel: 021 872 0686
Fax: 021 872 0534
info@capewinelands.org
www.capewinelands.org

Stellenbosch Tourist Office
Tel: 021 883 3584/9633
Fax: 021 883 8017
eikestad@iafrica.com
www.istellenbosch.org.za

Helderberg Tourism
Tel: 021 851 4022
Fax: 021 851 1497
info@helderbergtourism.co.za
www.helderbergtourism.co.za

Franschhoek Publicity
Tel: 021 876 3603
Fax: 021 876 2768
info@franschhoek.org.za
www.franschhoek.org.za

Paarl Publicity Association
Tel: 021 872 3829
Fax: 021 872 9376
paarl@cis.co.za
www.paarlonline.com

KWV, Paarl (cellar tours)
Tel: 021 807 3007/8
Fax: 021 807 3119
thewineemporium@kwv.co.za
www.kwv.co.za

Paarl Wine Route Office
Tel: 021 872 3605

Stellenbosch Wine Route Office
Tel: 021 886 4310
Fax: 021 886 4330
info@wineroute.co.za
www.wineroute.co.za

Vignerons de Franschhoek (tasting centres)
Tel: 021 876 3062
Fax: 021 876 2964
franschhoek@wine.co.za
www.franschhoekwines.co.za

Breede River Valley Tourism
Tel: 023 347 6411
Fax: 023 347 1115
manager@breederivervalley.co.za
www.breederivervalley.co.za

Western Wilderness

The West Coast and Cederberg

The coastal 'sandveld' strip north of Cape Town, bounded by the cool waters of the Atlantic Ocean and, in the east, by the towering heights of the Cederberg range, is an increasingly popular tourist region. It is the location of one of South Africa's newer and more beautiful national parks, of farmlands that yield fine crops of wheat, subtropical fruits and citrus, tobacco, vegetables, and grapes for both the table and the wine bottle. Delicious crayfish, or rock lobster, is a speciality of the seaboard areas; in springtime, the ephemeral wild flowers transform the countryside into a riot of colour.

The West Coast and Cederberg

West Coast National Park, Cederberg Wilderness Area

It is a fairly short, easy trip from Cape Town north to two of the Cape's most splendid tourist attractions. Assuming you want to explore both destinations on the same trip, you can take the R27, which leads you up the western seaboard to Langebaan and Velddrif. At Velddrif turn east towards Piketberg and then north on the N7 highway to Citrusdal, gateway to the magnificent Cederberg range. Alternatively, take the N7, turning west just before Piketberg for the coast or continue straight on to Citrusdal.

TOP *Langebaan Lagoon, haven for a myriad birds and, in spring, for a riot of wild flowers.*
ABOVE *Salt marsh at Langebaan.*
PREVIOUS PAGES *The Cederberg's Maltese Cross.*

WEST COAST NATIONAL PARK

Sandveld thickets, great carpets of springtime wild flowers, and one of the world's more important wetlands are protected within the almost 30 000-hectare West Coast National Park. So too are the shallow, limpid waters of Langebaan Lagoon, which stretches 16 kilometres across the dry, sometimes bleak-looking, treeless countryside to the coastal village of Yzerfontien in the south.

The park, its lagoon, mud- and sand-banks and and the offshore islands of Malgas (home to a huge colony of Cape gannets), Schaapen, Jutten and Marcus are a bird-lover's paradise, providing sanctuary and breeding grounds for more than 750 000 sea birds. Each summer, tens of thousands of migrant waders and water birds, including curlew sandpipers, knots and sanderlings, leave their Siberian and other Arctic breeding grounds to take the long journey south; many of them spending the warm months in and around the lagoon.

Bird hides are strategically placed around the reserve. There's an excellent one at the Geelbek Environmental and Education Centre, which is housed in a graceful old homestead built in 1860. There are wonderful views from here over the lagoon.

A number of important archaeological finds have been unearthed in the park,

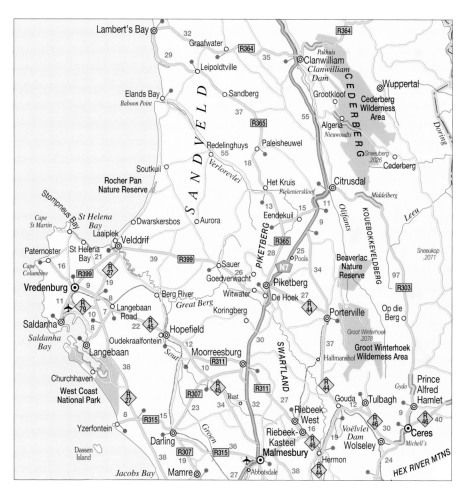

including fossils that date back some 10 million years. A more recent discovery is a pair of fossilised (and scientifically important) footprints made by an early modern human, estimated to be 117 000 years old. You need special permission to view the archaeological sites.

Apart from the fantastic birding and hiking opportunities, other facilities and activities in the park include fishing, sailing and other watersports. Accommodation is available in a houseboat moored on the lagoon, and at the nearby town of Langebaan (actually, a village), at Club Mykonos, a sophisticated Mediterranean-style hotel, timeshare and resort complex just to the north of the lagoon, in the nearby port town of Saldanha and, for those on environmental courses, at Geelbek.

On offer are self-guided and conducted walks, from Langebaan Lodge – the park's heaquarters and display centre – to the salt marshes and driftsand areas, three-day educational trails (from Geelbek), tours to the bird islands, canoeing and horseback trails, and a number of good swimming beaches.

The northern part of the park is occupied by the Postberg Nature Reserve, whose sandy terrain is enlivened by a sensational profusion of wild flowers in the brief springtime months. It is also haven to a number of animals, among them eland, bontebok, wildebeest, springbok, gemsbok, and kudu, all reintroduced to the area. There's a network of flower- and game-viewing roads, and some pleasant picnic sites. The Postberg section is open only during the flower season.

CEDERBERG WILDERNESS AREA

The large and lovely Olifants River, which has its source in the Cederberg

range, nurtures the citrus orchards around the town of Citrusdal and those of the wider area. They provide much of the wealth of this immensely fertile region. It's tourism focus, though, is the high and scenically superb mountains of the Cederberg just to the east.

TOP LEFT Flowers bloom everywhere, even on the beaches.
BELOW Provided the winter rains are good, wild flowers in their millions carpet the western coastal strip.

ABOVE Mosses proliferate in the Cederberg's wetlands.
BELOW The Cederberg wilderness is distinguished by its weirdly weathered sandstone formations.
BOTTOM RIGHT One of the Postberg's stranger rock formations.

Soaring peaks, rugged ridges, pristine natural vegetation and some of the weirdest rock formations you'll see anywhere are features of the 72 000-hectare Cederberg Wilderness Area.

For nature-lovers and hikers, the Cederberg is a dream. There's an excellent system of paths and trails, and a number of camping sites, basic shelter in overnight huts, and more up-market accommodation in self-catering cottages. No fires are allowed (other than in designated barbecue areas). A permit to enter the wilderness area must be obtained from the Cederberg Wilderness Authority or the Cape Nature Conservation offices.

The Cederberg can be baking hot on summer days, bitterly cold on winter nights. Snow mantles the higher ground in the cold months, creating spectacular vistas, especially towards the 2 030-metre-high Sneeuberg, the loftiest of the peaks.

Algeria Forest Camp
Most day-visitors to the Cederberg stay at the large, well-appointed and attractively situated Algeria Forest Camp, easily reached from the main N7 highway between Citrusdal and Clanwilliam.

One of the wilderness area's most popular trails is the 37-kilometres, four- or five-day route that leaves from Algeria to zigzag steeply up to the Middelberg

overnight hut, passing by Cathedral Rocks, Grootlandsvlakte and the Wildehoutdrif River on its way to the Crystal Pools hut. If you're energetic, you can climb the Sneeuberg before continuing on to the Sleepad hut. From here it is an easy hike along Die Trap to Welbedacht Cave, leaving plenty of time to climb Tafelberg. The final day of the hike involves a short descent along Welbedacht gully.

Arches, Caves and Cracks
Among the Cederberg's most striking rock formations are the Wolfberg Arch, a 30-metre feature forged in a wall of rock, the Wolfberg Cracks (the main crack is a 30-metre cleft in the rockface), the 20-metre tall Maltese Cross, and Tafelberg – at 1 969 metres the second highest of the peaks. The Arch and Cracks can be explored from the Dwarsrivier Farm, as can the famed Stadsaal Caves and Elephant Cave, which contain some excellent San (Bushman) rock art. Permits and a key to the caves' gate can be obtained at the Dwarsrivier Farm.

The Stadsaal Caves and Elephant Cave are a short drive from Sanddrif, on both the Driehoek River and the road to Matjiesrivier, but it is a hefty hike and climb to reach the Cracks (a four- to five-hour round trip). It takes 45 minutes from Sanddrif to the Arch, and it's a day-hike

to the Maltese Cross. Incidentally, there is also a short walk from Sanddrif to the most exquisite of natural dams.
It's filled with boulders over and around which small waterfalls tumble.

Be warned that it is very difficult to observe and enjoy these features from a distance, because of the nature of the land and its multitude of twisted rock formations. You have to wait till you're virtually on top of them. So be prepared to endure a tough journey, and make sure that you have plenty of provisions (especially water). The end result, however, is well worth the effort.

Plants and Animals

The Cederberg takes its name from the groves of the Clanwillian cedar trees (*Widdringtonia cederbergensis*) that occur in patches on the rocky outcrops and mountain tops. The species, once plentiful, was almost wiped out by indiscriminate woodcutting, and by veld fires, until a rescue operation was launched some time ago. Another of the Cederberg's specialities is the rare, endemic, cup-shaped snow protea (*Protea*

cryophila), a high-altitude plant that clings precariously to life on the rocky ledges above the snow line. The plant flowers between January and April, mainly in February.

The Cederberg provides ideal habitats for Cape grysbok, grey rhebok, common duiker, klipspringer and chacma baboon, and the entire wilderness was recently declared a leopard conservation area, although you are unlikely to see these shy, mostly nocturnal animals.

ABOVE The rugged uplands of the Cederberg: a paradise for hikers and nature-lovers.

USEFUL CONTACTS

Postberg Nature Reserve has magnificent views over Langebaan Lagoon.

West Coast Tourism
Tel: 022 433 2380
Fax: 022 433 2172
tourism@capewestcoast.org
www.capewestcoast.org

South African National Parks
Tel: 012 428 9111
Fax: 012 343 0905
reservations@parks-sa.co.za
www.parks-sa.co.za

Flowerline
Cell: 083 910 1028

West Coast National Park
Tel: 022 772 2144
Fax: 022 772 2607
www.parks-sa.co.za

Clanwilliam Tourism
Tel: 027 482 2024
Fax: 027 482 2361
cederberg@lando.co.za
www.capewestcoast.org

Cederberg Wilderness Area
Tel: 027 482 2812
Fax: 027 482 2406
cedeberg@cnc.org.za
www.cederberg.co.za

Painted Deserts

Namaqualand, the Richtersveld and the Kalahari

Southern Africa's western and west-central regions are not blessed by good rainfall. Most are classed as 'arid wilderness', some parts are classic desert country. But they support an astonishing diversity of living forms and each, in its own way, has its beauty. Namaqualand is famed for the glory of its springtime wild flowers; the Richtersveld for its strikingly unusual landscapes and unique plant life; the Kalahari for its far horizons and desert-adapted animals. And each welcomes the visitor who chooses the 'big country' and its lonely spaces over the more comfortable, more conventional tourist routes.

Namaqualand, the Richtersveld and the Kalahari

Namaqualand, Richtersveld National Park, Augrabies Falls National Park, Kgalagadi Transfrontier Park.

The highway from Cape Town – the N7 – runs straight and true northwards through Namaqualand to the Orange River, which hugs the Richtersveld National Park in the broad bend of its lower reaches. For the Kalahari, branch off eastwards on the N14 at Springbok. It's a long and lonely road to Augrabies and the town of Upington, at which point you turn north on the R360 for the Kgalagadi Transfrontier Park.

TOP The Skilpad reserve is one of the region's floral 'hotspots'.
ABOVE An angulate tortoise plods through the spring flowers.
PREVIOUS PAGES In spring, Namaqualand becomes a vast flower garden.

NAMAQUALAND

The region known as Namaqualand – named for its early Nama inhabitants – roughly encompasses that strip of land that is bound by the Olifants River in the south, runs along the Atlantic Ocean to the west, across the bleak Richtersveld region in the north, and into the rugged, largely empty region of Bushmanland in the east. Each spring – usually between mid-August and mid-October – this semi-desert area is transformed into one of the world's most colourful natural displays as small hardy low-growing plants burst into flower.

Seeds of the mesembryanthemums (locally called *vygies*) lie dormant over the long, dry summer months.

But after moderate winter rains, and within a matter of days, the landscape is covered in great carpets of purple, yellow, orange and white blossoms. And it is not just the small plants that rush to flower. The aloes, flax, lilies, azalias, perennial herbs and other species of the region add their bright hues to the intricate tapestry.

The flowers usually reach their brilliant best towards the end of August, but because different species have slightly different flowering timetables, Namaqualand is ablaze with colour for weeks on end during the spring period.

The ideal time of day to view the displays is between about eleven in the morning and three in the afternoon, when the flowers are fully open, turning their faces to the sun.

It is possible to enjoy the spectacle through the car window, but probably more rewarding to visit one or other of the region's several delightful nature reserves, where the blooms are in especially striking profusion, and where you can explore the vistas on foot. It is suggested you contact the destination of your choice or Flowerline (see p. 143) before setting out on the long drive, just

to make sure that the journey will indeed be worthwhile.

If you do decide to take your chances and simply drive through Namaqualand, stop at any of the small desert villages off the N7 freeway – such as Garies, Kamieskroon, Hondeklipbaai and Springbok – to view the magnificent floral mantle for which the area is so well known. All the towns have a central office from where you can obtain information on the best viewing spots.

Wild Flower Reserves

The delightful 1 000-hectare Skilpad Wildflower Reserve is situated to the south of Springbok, near Kamieskroon on the first ridge of hills separating the interior from the coast. The reserve is open only during the flower season.

Goegap Nature Reserve, covering 15 000 hectares of granitic hills and sandy flats 15 kilometres southeast of Springbok, hosts more than 600 indigenous flower species. The area is also haven to a number of different types of mammal, including Hartmann's mountain zebra, eland, klipspringer and the yellow mongoose. Within the Goegap Reserve, the Hester Malan Wild Flower Garden showcases many of Namaqualand's succulent plants in its delightful rock garden.

Further south, near Calvinia, is the small Akkerdam Nature Reserve, and you'll find the 900-hectare bird-rich Rocher Pan Nature Reserve about 25 kilometres north of Velddrif.

THE RICHTERSVELD

The northern reaches of the Northern Cape Province are semi-deserts, desolate and sparsely populated. The Richtersveld National Park, embraced by the crook of the Orange River as it bends into Namibia, is no exception.

But hot and dry though they may be, the landscapes are memorable in their awesome starkness – the 162 500-hectare park is a surrealistic blend of broad, bone-dry sandy plains and crenellated lava mountains that majestically twist and fault.

To get to the park from Cape Town, travel straight up the N7 to Springbok. The entrance is still another 300-odd

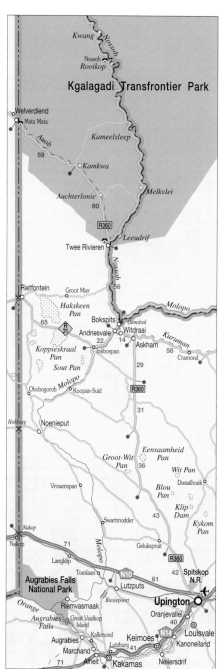

ABOVE *The succulent halfmens (left) and quiver tree (right) in the Goegap Reserve.*

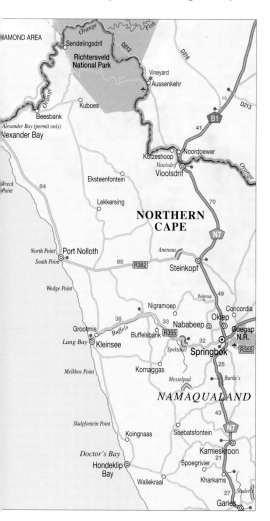

TOP *The Richtersveld is not for the faint-hearted; those that make the effort, though, are treated to awe-inspiring scenery.* ABOVE *Tiny, stone-like lithops species are distinctive to the dry Richtersveld.* BELOW *Orange River rafters.*

kilometres from here via Steinkopf, Port Nolloth and Alexander Bay, or via Steinkopf, Viooldrif and Rosyntjieberg. Only high-clearance and 4x4 vehicles (no caravans) can manage the rocky terrain and crude gravel roads. Indeed, sedan cars are not even permitted entry.

To the eye, the Richtersveld terrain seems bleak, forbidding, largely barren, but in reality it is a botanist and nature-lover's paradise.

The park is home to some 30 per cent of all South Africa's succulent plant species, many of which belong to the mesembryanthemum group. Among other plants are the bizarre halfmens (half-man) or elephant-trunk tree, the quiver tree, the maiden's quiver tree or bush tree, and the eight-day miracle grass, which, in order to survive the harsh climate, germinates, flowers and runs to seed all within just eight days of rain.

There's not much to see in terms of wildlife, except a surprisingly prolific array of desert-adapted reptiles, and insect species that have evolved specialist survival strategies against the harsh desert environment. Mammals found in the area include the occasional klipspringer, grey rhebok, Hartmann's mountain zebra, kudu and, rarely, leopard. The park is, however, fairly rich in bird life, with some 200 recorded species, including the African fish eagle.

Richtersveld National Park is a 'contractual' conservation area, which means it is managed jointly by South African National Parks and the local community – the Nama people, most of whom are poor goatherds whose lives have remained relatively unchanged for hundreds of years.

Entry and fishing permits can be obtained from the headquarters and reception office at Sendelingsdrif, where there is also a guest cottage. Within the park itself there are a few designated camping sites – at Richtersberg, Kokerboomkloof, Potjiespram, Die Koei and De Hoop – but none offers any facilities, shelter, or even water. So a visit to the park should be well planned. Make sure that you are equipped with everything you need for the length of your stay – fuel, spares, food, water (and insect repellent) – before entering.

Because of the harsh terrain and the remoteness of the area, it is recommended that, for mutual assistance, vehicles travel in convoy.

Despite its intimidating nature, the Richtersveld is a splendid area to explore on foot, although hiking is permitted only with an official guide. Depending on the season, the park can be either incredibly hot or bitterly cold during the day. Night-time temperatures are generally very cool.

Take proper precautions against both the sun and the chill. Malaria prophylactics are advised.

THE ORANGE RIVER

The Orange River was known to the early settlers in the region as the Gariep, or 'Great River'. It has its source in the Maloti Mountains of Lesotho, far away to the east, from where it flows westwards on its 2 250-kilometre journey across the subcontinent, plunging over the Augrabies Gorge before making its way over the last, desolate stretch to the Atlantic seaboard between the diamond centres of Oranjemund (in Namibia) and Alexander Bay.

Orange River Canoe Trails

One of the most exciting ways of exploring the region is on a water safari, in a canoe, raft, kayak or inflatable 'rubber duck', paddling over long stretches of the wide river as it winds along the border of the park.

You can either take your own craft, or join one of the canoe safaris (these

ABOVE The De Hoop camp site, on the banks of the Orange River, is a popular overnight stop.
BELOW The dawn sun brings brilliant colour to the Orange River.

TOP AND ABOVE At times, the river at Augrabies Falls is a relative trickle, at others a raging torrent as it roars through the 18-kilometre-long canyon.
BELOW Springbok are completely acclimatised to desert conditions.

must be booked in advance). A popular river run is that through the moonscape of the park's northern section, which for the most part makes its way between Noordoewer, on the main road crossing, and the Fish River Junction – an excursion that is both exhilarating and safe.

Canoe safari tours are operated on various sections of the river, and generally range from three to six days, covering about 20 kilometres a day. Groups comprise between 15 and 30 trailists, and the trails cater for pretty well everyone, although participants should be good swimmers and reasonably fit.

Canoeing, camping and safety equipment are all provided by tour operators, many of whom will also – depending on the operator and group 's requirements – supply food and handle the catering side. Rapids along most sections are graded between 1 and 6, which means that they range from the gentle to the downright impossible to negotiate. The latter must be skirted on foot or by vehicle.

THE ROUTE EAST

There is a route that leads east from the Richtersveld park to Upington, but if you're coming from Cape Town and your destination is the Augrabies Falls National Park and, beyond, the Kgalagadi Transfrontier Park, it's better to turn off the N7 at Springbok and follow the N14 highway. Turn off again just before the town of Kakamas and continue for just under 30 kilometres to Augrabies. To reach the vast desert reserve of the Kgalagadi, carry on along the N14 (past the Augrabies turn-off) to Upington. From here, take the R360 northwards to the park.

AUGRABIES FALLS NATIONAL PARK

Augrabies was known as Aukoerabis, or 'The Place of Great Noise', by the early Khoi people – and very apt the name is, too.

Here, during the summer flood, the mighty Orange River crashes over the rim of a canyon to plunge 190 metres, over terraces of smooth granite, in a dramatic

multi-stream waterfall that, in terms of volume, is South Africa's largest and the world's sixth largest. During its course it thunders through an 18-kilometre-long gorge carved into the rock over a period of 500 million years.

The park itself extends across 88 000 hectares – a true wilderness, striking in its arid, lunar landscapes, and there is much to be seen. It is, among other things, a refuge for one of Africa's rarest animals, the black rhino. Here, too, you'll find giraffe and antelope such as klipspringer, and some 200 different kinds of bird.

Plant life includes an incredible number of succulent species.

Hikes through the park vary in length from an hour to several days, depending on your preferences and time available. There are also mountain-biking, canoe and 4x4 routes that include the Aukoerabis 4x4 Eco-trail and the Black Rhino Adventure Trail (whose focus, obviously, is the scarce black rhino).

Recommended is a drive to one or more of the lookout points, which offer spectacular views of the gorge below the falls. Organised night drives from the reception office (at the main camp site) during peak season are extremely popular. For day visitors who just want to take the short detour off the N14 – to look at the falls, perhaps enjoy an alfresco meal and then press on with their journey. There is a nice picnic spot near the camp site and reception.

Accommodation in the park is at Augrabies Falls Rest Camp, a pleasant collection of self-catering chalets, cottages and bungalows. There are also caravan and camping sites located in pretty, shaded areas. The rest camp has swimming pools, a restaurant, shop, pub and grill.

KGALAGADI TRANSFRONTIER PARK

The giant Kgalagadi, the first of the continent's cross-border 'peace parks', is the product of a visionary agreement between South Africa and Botswana. Although the two segments have never,

TOP LEFT This diminutive klipspringer, standing on tiptoe atop a rocky outcrop, keeps a watchful eye open for predators. ABOVE One of Kgalagadi's huge black-maned lions – a real tourist drawcard. BELOW Black rhino eke out a living on the Augrabies' sparse vegetation. The remote countryside, nevertheless, is an ideal habitat – partly because predatory poachers can be kept at bay.

ABOVE Hardy camel thorns are among the few trees that grow in the arid Kgalagadi. BELOW Kgalagadi San (Bushmen) ply their crafts to passing tourists.

for the most part, been physically separated by fences, the political and administrative barriers between South Africa's Kalahari Gemsbok National Park and the Gemsbok National Park of Botswana have been removed, allowing the two to be run as an integrated entity. The game animals range freely between them. The combined area is the first of Africa's ground-breaking 'peace' parks.

The Kgalagadi covers almost a million hectares of red sand dunes and semi-desert savannah. The dry river beds of the Auob and Nossob are vegetated with hardy dryland species such as camel thorn, raisin-bush and shepherd's tree.

Although the Kgalagadi is much larger than (almost twice as large, actually) the Kruger National Park, it cannot compete in terms of the diversity of its animals, birds and, most especially, its plants. But the wildlife is both plentiful, and fascinating in the way much of it has adapted to the harsh desert conditions. The park is haven to 58 mammal, 55 reptile and 260 bird species (including 20 different kinds of raptor) and a vast array

of insects. Social weavers are found throughout the region, their massive nests, often built in camel-thorn trees, a common sight. Herds of antelope such as eland, springbok, blue wildebeest and red hartebeest, as well groups of spotted hyenas and black-backed jackals, survive and sometimes thrive in this sandy, inhospitable land.

The park's annual recorded rainfall averages just 350 millimetres, and precipitation is unpredictable and unevenly distributed.

Lack of surface water and the long months of drought that dry up the pans force the animals and birds to depend, for much of the time, on man-made water holes (boreholes) and on the indigenous tsamma melons and Kalahari cucumbers for their life-giving moisture requirements.

Two of the park's animals are rather special, namely the superbly adapted gemsbok (which gave the park its original name), and the famed black-maned Kalahari lion. Also present are leopards and cheetahs, porcupines, honey badgers,

bat-eared foxes and the inquisitive little mongoose known locally as the meerkat. The cheetahs are especially notable. These sleek and swift animals, among Africa's most endangered, flourish in the open country, and because vegetation is so sparse, they offer the visitor superb viewing.

There are three overnight camps within the Park – Twee Rivieren, Nossob and Mata Mata. All offer accommodation and fuel, and have shops that sell basic commodities. Twee Rivieren's shop is the only one to stock fresh meat, eggs, bread and margarine. Fresh fruit and vegetables are not available.

Twee Rivieren is the main camp, and is situated at the confluence of the Nossob and Auob rivers. It offers game and night drives, the latter – a very popular excursion – departing each evening at about seven-thirty in summer (earlier in winter). Twee Rivieren has a restaurant and swimming pool.

Kgalagadi Four-by-Four Trails

Kgalagadi offers a number of four-wheel-drive excursions, including the superb Nossob 4x4 Trail, which can be booked in advance at Twee Rivieren. The route takes you from the camp northwards for about 170 kilometres, passing more than 20 man-made water holes (excellent game-viewing spots) and ending at the Nossob Rest Camp. The road sometimes

runs within and sometimes alongside the river bed. The rugged Gemsbok Wilderness Trail (which is, in fact, suitable only for 4x4 vehicles) leads into the heart of Botswana's incomparable wilderness. It runs for 257 kilometres on a dirt track, from a point some 55 kilometres north of Nossob, and ends just north of Ljiersdraal, also on the Nossob road.

From Nossob it is possible to keep going for a further 120 kilometres to the seriously remote hamlet of Union's End. Lions are said to be plentiful north of the Nossob camp, especially near the Kwang water hole. Kwang, situated some 20 kilometres from the Nossob, also attracts great numbers of antelope.

Another, shorter 4x4 trail runs to the northwest of Twee Rivieren (the trail has been upgraded) and 130 kilometres along the Auob River. Wildlife enthusiasts claim that this is one of the best places in the world to see cheetah on the hunt.

At present, the Botswana side of the Park has very few facilities. There are camping grounds at Two Rivers, Rooiputs and Polentswa, but you need to take your own water and supplies.

TOP LEFT Massive social weavers' nests festoon the region's trees.
ABOVE The red sands of the Kalahari.

USEFUL CONTACTS

South African National Parks
For information and bookings
Tel: 012 428 9111
Fax: 012 343 0905
reservations@parks-sa.co.za
www.parks-sa.co.za

Northern Cape Tourism Authority
Tel: 053 832 2657
Fax: 053 831 2937
tourism@northerncape.co.za
www.northerncape.org.za

Flowerline
Cell (toll-free, July-October):
083 910 1028

Namaqualand Regional Tourism Office
Tel: 027 712 2011
Fax: 027 712 1421
namakwaland@intekom.co.za
www.northerncape.org.za

Richtersveld National Park
Tel: 027 831 1506

Augrabies Falls National Park
Tel: 054 452 9200

Kgalagadi Transfrontier Park
Tel: 054 561 2000

Twee Rivieren tourist accommodation.

Chalet at Augrabies Falls National Park.

Folios in **bold** typeface represent illustrated pages